Reading
the Synoptic
Gospels

Reading the Synoptic Gospels

Basic Methods for Interpreting
Matthew, Mark, and Luke

O. Wesley Allen, Jr.

Chalice Press.
St. Louis, Missouri

Bible quotations, unless otherwise noted, are from the *New Revised Standard Version Bible,* copyright 1989, Division of Christian Education of the National Council of the Churches of Christ in the United States of America. Used by permission. All rights reserved.

Excerpts from *The New Jerusalem Bible,* copyright 1985 by Darton, Longman & Todd, Ltd., and Doubleday, a division of Bantam Doubleday Dell Publishing Group, Inc. Used by permission.

The Revised English Bible copyright © Oxford University Press and Cambridge University Press 1989. The Revised English Bible with the Apocrypha first published 1989. The Revised English Bible is a revision of the New English Bible: The New English Bible New Testament was first published by the Oxford and Cambridge University Presses in 1961, and the complete Bible in 1970.

New American Bible Scripture texts and prefaces used in the work constitute the New American Bible with Revised Psalms and Revised New Testament, copyright © 1986. 1991 by the Confraternity of Christian Doctrine, 3211 Fourth Street, N.E., Washington, D.C. 20017. All rights reserved. The text of the Old Testament in the New American Bible with Revised Psalms and Revised New Testament was published in the New American Bible, copyright © 1970 by the Confraternity of Christian Doctrine (Books from 1 Samuel to 2 Maccabees inclusive copyright © 1969). All rights reserved. No part of the New American Bible with Revised Psalms and Revised New Testament may be reproduced in any form without permission in writing from the copyright owner.

Nihil obstat: Stephen J. Haridegen, O.F. M., S.S.L. and Christian P. Ceroke. O. Carm., S.T.D.

Imprimatur: Patrick Cardinal O'Boyle, D.D., Archbishop of Washington, July 27, 1970. The Revised Psalms

Imprimatur: Most Reverend Daniel E. Pilarczyk, President, National Conference of Catholic Bishops, September 10, 1991.

Cover art: Simone Cantarini, detail of "Saint Matthew and the Angel," gift of James Belden in memory of Evelyn Berry Belden. Photograph © 1999 Board of Trustees, National Gallery of Art, Washington, D.C.
Cover design: Scott Tjaden
Art director: Elizabeth Wright
Interior design: Wynn Younker

This book is printed on acid-free, recycled paper.

Visit Chalice Press on the World Wide Web at
www.chalicepress.com

10 9 8 7 6 5 4 3 2 1   00 01 02 03 04 05

Library of Congress Cataloging—in—Publication Data

Allen, O. Wesley, 1965–
    Reading the synoptic gospels: basic methods for interpreting Matthew,   Mark, and Luke / by O. Wesley Allen, Jr.
        p. cm.
    Includes bibliographical references.
    ISBN 0-8272-3219-5
    1. Bible. N.T. Gospels—Hermeneutics. 2. Bible. N.T. Gospels—Criticism, interpretation, etc.   I. Title
    BS2555.2 .A44 200
    226'.06'01—dc21   99-049162

Printed in the United States of America

For my daughter Maggie

CONTENTS

Preface

Most undergraduate New Testament introduction textbooks and courses spend so much time (as they must) explaining what the New Testament says and the context in which its works were originally written that almost no time is left to teach the exegetical process of reading the New Testament. Students learn about critical issues dealing with the study of the historical Jesus or the theology of Paul, but are rarely given the necessary tools to continue the critical, interpretive process on their own. I have written this book out of a belief that it is important for students being introduced to a critical reading of the Bible to also be introduced to the methodology of critically reading the Bible for themselves. Therefore, this work is not in itself an introduction to the full range of gospel studies, but is intended to serve as a text supplementing a broader introductory study of the gospels or the New Testament in the classroom or church.

Many people have helped in the shaping and production of this work. First and foremost are the students I have encountered at Candler School of Theology at Emory University, Georgia State University, Interdenominational Theological Center, Georgia Institute of Technology, and DePauw University. They have been generous in their feedback as this material was tested in lecture, seminar, and manuscript forms. A special thanks needs to be expressed to Roy Wells at Birmingham-Southern College. He not only read the manuscript and offered scholarly advice that made the work much better, he tested the material on synoptic gospels classes, and was able to offer practical advice.

Many have offered aid in the actual writing and production of the book and deserve recognition. They have helped raise the quality of the book in significant ways. Two seminary students who have been especially helpful in proofreading and offering critical suggestions are Matthew McLaughlin (Boston University) and Bryan Brooks (Emory University)—I have tried to honor them appropriately later in the book. Two colleagues and friends at DePauw who have assisted in the final editing and production of the text are Bob Eccles and Deborah Chew. And, of course, I could not appreciate more the support, encouragement, and patience I have received from the Chalice Press staff, especially David Polk.

I must also acknowledge that if there is anything in this book worth sharing with students of the New Testament, it is, to a great degree, due to the quality education I received at the hands of biblical scholars at Birmingham-Southern College, Yale Divinity School, and Emory University. They taught me not only how to interpret scripture but also *why* to interpret scripture. I hope this book in some way measures up to the example of excellence they set for me.

And, finally and most importantly, for supporting me as I toiled and for pushing me when I did not toil hard enough, I am most thankful to and for my wife, Bonnie Cook.

Introduction

How Hard Can It Be?

Anyone who has ever attended a Bible study or listened to a sermon is likely to have heard the expression, "What this scripture passage means to me is…" Is it any wonder then that the common assumption among readers of the Bible is that the meaning of scripture is easily accessible? The impression given is that all that is required to interpret any passage is reading and personal reflection. A scriptural passage may have other meanings for other people, but it means this "to me." In such a view of scripture the author, or perhaps God, is seen as speaking directly to the reader in a manner and with a message that is easily discernible.

This book is dedicated to the idea that layers of meanings in scripture are indeed accessible to anyone who is willing to read the biblical writings. It is also based, however, on the recognition that there is nothing simple or easy about the process of discovering those layers of meaning. Interpreting scripture with depth is hard work. Reading must give way to study. And reflection must incorporate research. The meanings in any piece of literature (including the biblical writings) that are worth discovering, expounding, and claiming as one's own are rarely those found at the surface level. One must search over and over again to find the true treasures hidden in such a field of meaning.

Or, to shift metaphors slightly, an interpreter must approach a biblical text as an archaeologist approaches a dig, slowly and

1

carefully removing layer after layer of dirt to find artifacts that have been buried for centuries. Imagine an archaeological site at which are found, twenty feet below the surface, remnants from late Byzantine times. Thirty feet down are found remains from the first century C.E. (Common Era). Forty-five feet down, evidence of a third century B.C.E. (Before the Common Era), pre–Roman Empire civilization is found. And so on. If one had never dug, the only experience of the site would have been that of a grassy mound. Only by meticulously digging deeper and deeper in stages is one able to experience the full history and significance of the place. Interpretation of scripture is likewise an attempt to uncover various layers of meaning by carefully researching the passage under investigation. This takes time and work (yes, work—you know, the whole inspiration-perspiration thing) but is worth the effort when an old, familiar passage is found to be filled with new and different meanings than had been previously recognized.

Exegesis

In an "Introduction to the Old Testament" course at Yale Divinity School, Professor Brevard Childs was assigning a paper in which students were to interpret a passage from Genesis. After describing what we students believed to be the most important elements of the assignment—how many pages were required, what size margins were expected, the number of sources to be consulted, and when it was due—Professor Childs offered one last caveat. To paraphrase: "To interpret scripture better, you must become a deeper person." The saying is true. The ability to discover the depth of meanings in scripture is in direct correlation with the intellectual, emotional, and spiritual depth of the readers themselves.

However, the reverse is also true for people of the Book: To become a deeper person, you must interpret scripture better. When people of faith read scripture, they do not do so primarily as literary critics or historians, nor do they read simply to be entertained. People of faith read scripture as part of their search to correct and expand their view of the world, of self, and of that which is Ultimate, because, in their faith stance, they have granted scripture some sort of an authoritative voice in this search.

A surface reading of scripture is unable to bring about a true transformation or expansion of one's views of reality. Simply reading for "what this means to me" is little more than license to import the views we already hold *into* the text. This is like archaeologists who find an ancient oil lamp and, based on their own modern cultural experience, claim, "It looks like an ashtray to us." Reading scripture in this fashion is often called *eisegesis* (pronounced eis-uh-JEE-sis) from the Greek, meaning "to lead (*ago*) into (*eis*)."

Traditionally, the process of discovering meaning below the surface in biblical texts has been referred to as *exegesis* (pronounced ex-uh-JEE-sis). The Greek root of *exegesis*, of course, means "to lead (*ago*) out (*ex*)." Exegesis consists of using methods of reading (i.e., asking certain types of questions) to draw deeper meanings *out of* the text and to avoid forcing meaning into the text. The person seeking an informed interpretation of texts will want to use exegetical (pronounced ex-uh-JEH-ti-kuhl) methods to structure the experience of a biblical passage.

No matter what critical, exegetical methodologies we use, however, we should not buy into an illusion that our reading is an objective interpretation. Every reading is subjective in the sense that the way we use interpretive methodologies is shaped by who we are and why we are interpreting a text. *Who we are:* Am I reading as a person of faith or as a scholar interested in historically significant documents? How do my gender, socioeconomic status, and ethnicity bias the way I read? What communities have influenced the way I read: ecclesiastical, educational, geographical, and so on? How does my twentieth/twenty-first century, scientific worldview influence my response to ancient, prescientific texts? What kind of political being am I, and what presuppositions does that orientation carry with it? *Why we are interpreting:* Is this process meant to inform personal religious study? Am I interpreting a synoptic passage on behalf of or to be communicated to others (e.g., a Sunday school class, congregation, college seminar, or professor)? Am I a student presenting an interpretation to be graded by a teacher or am I an "authority" figure (such as a preacher or teacher) offering my interpretation to a group for instruction? How will my interpretation be presented to these others (e.g., lecture, dialogue, or written essay)? Regardless of who we are and why we are interpreting a passage, using exegetical methodologies helps to keep our subjective tendencies in check. An interpretation will always be *my* interpretation, but my interpretation will be informed by *shared*, critical, exegetical principles.

Scope of This Introduction

While everyone who has ever read a part of the Bible has played the role of interpreter, exegesis has primarily been an exercise reserved for scholars and clergy (although clergy often forget the emphasis placed on exegesis in their seminary training and revert to eisegesis in their preaching and teaching). In order to narrow the gap between the Church and the Academy, this volume introduces those exegetical methods prevalent in the academic setting that are most accessible and most useful to new students of exegesis. The methods presented here are by no means all the methods biblical scholars use in their study. Other methods, however, require a level of sophisticated engagement with linguistic, historical, literary, and ideological theories that is beyond the scope of this introduction. Moreover, the methods introduced in this book can and should be studied in greater depth, mastered with greater proficiency, and used in conjunction with the study of biblical languages. This book is simply an attempt to offer students their first glance at the archaeologist's tools so that they will have some of the skills necessary to *begin* digging deeper into biblical texts.

Each method we introduce approaches biblical texts from a different perspective and thus investigates different layers of meaning in those texts. Nevertheless, these methods overlap, as do the layers of meaning they investigate. Therefore, we view the individual methods not as ends in themselves, but as interlinking steps in a process of interpretation. (Indeed, as one becomes more proficient and comfortable with exegesis, the steps will become merged into a more cohesive, less mechanistic process than presented in this introduction.) The goal of the exegetical process is to develop one's own informed, holistic interpretation of a biblical passage for a particular context and purpose.

The way we read a text is determined in part by the type of material it represents. For instance, we do not study a newspaper the way we do a course textbook. We do not ponder its use of language the way we do poetry. We do not read it from beginning to end the way we do narrative. Likewise, we do not use identical methods when we read and interpret gospels, legal material, psalms, letters, proverbs, apocalypses, or prophetic oracles from the Bible. To introduce exegetical methods appropriate for all these types of biblical literature runs the risk of losing the focus of the interpretive process from beginning to end. Therefore, to keep our study manageable, we will examine exegetical methods as they are applied to the synoptic gospels (Matthew, Mark, and Luke). This focus does not mean that none of the skills learned in this study can be transferred to the task of interpreting other biblical texts. Many of the exegetical steps described in this book can be applied to, or are easily adapted to be used with, other biblical texts, especially other narrative materials. Still, they are described here as they specifically apply to the synoptic materials.

In order to focus our study even more sharply, we will illustrate the way the various methods work by applying each one to a single synoptic gospel passage instead of discussing the methods in relation to different passages or to the gospels in general. Our example passage is Matthew 12:46–50:

> [46]While he was still speaking to the crowds, his mother and his brothers were standing outside, wanting to speak to him. [47]Someone told him, "Look, your mother and your brothers are standing outside, wanting to speak to you." [48]But to the

one who had told him this, Jesus replied, "Who is my mother, and who are my brothers?" [49]And pointing to his disciples, he said, "Here are my mother and my brothers! [50]For whoever does the will of my Father in heaven is my brother and sister and mother."

By observing each method being applied to this single passage, we will be able to learn how the various methods work together and build on one another.

Additional Resources

Because most people who put their hand to the task of interpreting scripture do not have a theological library at their disposal, this study has been designed to introduce exegetical methodology that can be followed with minimal resources. But resources are needed. For the beginning student of gospel exegesis, the following are recommended:

Bible: There are many biblical translations and editions from which to choose. However, when we are looking for an edition that serves well for exegesis, our choices narrow. We need a translation that keeps a sound balance between being readable (i.e., translates the biblical languages into current idiomatic English) and being true to the original texts (i.e., maintains the flavor of the ancient world and thought). We need a recent edition that has used the most up-to-date biblical scholarship in its translation process. And, finally, it is helpful to have a volume that is annotated with short introductory and explanatory notes. The translation we recommend is the *New Revised Standard Version* (NRSV). The specific study Bible we use in this study is *HarperCollins Study Bible* (New York: HarperCollins, 1993). In this edition, scholars who are members of the largest guild of English-speaking biblical scholars (the Society of Biblical Literature [SBL]) have written introductions and notes for each biblical and apocryphal work.

Synopsis: A synopsis (from the Greek, meaning "seeing" [*optic*] "together/alike" [*syn*]) is a book that lays Matthew, Mark, and Luke (and sometimes John) side by side in parallel columns. This allows us to more easily compare and contrast the outlines and structures of the gospels in their entirety, as well as the content of their individual passages. We recommend and use in this introduction *Gospel Parallels*, edited by Burton H. Throckmorton, Jr. (Nashville: Thomas Nelson, 1992), especially since it uses the NRSV.

Concordance: A concordance is an index listing the occurrence of every word in the Bible. The one used in this study is John R. Kohlenberger, III's *The NRSV Concordance Unabridged* (Grand Rapids, Mich.: Zondervan, 1991). The problem with English concordances is that they index the English translation. If one looks up "love" in a concordance, there is no way to know which of the several Greek words meaning love is being represented. Analytical concordances overcome this problem by indicating Greek and Hebrew vocabulary being translated. These are more difficult to use, but the profit may be higher. One example is Richard E. Whitaker's *The Eerdmans Analytical Concordance to the RSV* (Grand Rapids, Mich.: Eerdmans, 1988). There are also numerous biblical computer programs that can perform word searches.

One-Volume Commentary: While commentaries on individual biblical works are able to comment on texts in much more depth, a one-volume commentary is an invaluable resource for beginning interpreters because it has notes on every piece of the Bible. I recommend *The Harper Bible Commentary*, edited by James L. Mays (San Francisco: Harper, 1988), because, like the *HarperCollins Study Bible*, it represents a joint project of scholars in the SBL. Some may prefer the Roman Catholic *New Jerome Bible Commentary*, edited by Raymond E. Brown, Joseph Fitzmyer, and Roland E. Murphy (Englewood Cliffs, N.J.: Prentice Hall, 1990).

One-Volume Bible Dictionary: Bible dictionaries are encyclopedic reference works that contain short essays on subject matter ranging from A to Z: Antioch, cubit, gestures, John, the Lord's Prayer, Passover, scroll, virtue, zealot. As with commentaries, a one-volume dictionary cannot do the job as well as multiple volumes (such as the *Anchor Bible Dictionary* or the older *Interpreter's Dictionary of the Bible*), but it is much less expensive and serves as a good starting point. We recommend *The HarperCollins Bible Dictionary*, edited by Paul J. Achtemeier, for it also is part of the joint project of scholars in the SBL. But many of its entries are far too brief.

For readers interested in moving beyond the introductory level of this book, we have provided suggestions for further reading at the end of each chapter.

For Further Reading

Baird, William. "Biblical Criticism." In *Anchor Bible Dictionary*, ed. David Noel Freedman, 1.725–36. New York: Doubleday, 1992.

Hayes, John H., and Carl R. Holladay. "Introducing Exegesis." In *Biblical Exegesis: A Beginner's Handbook*, rev. ed., 5–32. Atlanta: John Knox Press, 1987.

Stuart, Douglas. "Exegesis." In *Anchor Bible Dictionary*, ed. David Noel Freedman, 2.682–88. New York: Doubleday, 1992.

CHAPTER 1

Establishing the Pericope, Text, and Plain Sense

The gospel of Luke opens with a prologue that offers us some insight into the manner in which the gospel writers went about their task:

> [1]Since many have undertaken to set down an orderly account of the events that have been fulfilled among us, [2]just as they were handed on to us by those who from the beginning were eyewitnesses and servants of the word, [3]I too decided, after investigating everything carefully from the very first, to write an orderly account for you, most excellent Theophilus, [4]so that you may know the truth concerning the things about which you have been instructed. (Luke 1:1–4)

The author claims to have researched *events* in Christ's life by exploring various *accounts* of those events—his sources are eyewitnesses, servants of the word, and many orderly accounts (i.e., other gospels)—and then to have arranged his rendition of those events into an orderly account of his own. Assuming Luke is representative, the way the synoptic gospel writers operated was to collect short accounts of stories, sayings, and dialogues of Jesus Christ and paste them together into a larger narrative. (For a brief introduction to the stages of development of the synoptic gospels, see Excursus 1.) The most elementary section of the gospel text on which an interpreter focuses, therefore, is one of these short accounts of an individual event or saying.

Establishing the Pericope

Gospel scholars call one of these discrete passages a *pericope* (plural *pericopae*). The word is pronounced "puh-RIK-uh-pee" (not "periscope" without the "s," the way many think it is pronounced the first time they see the word in print). The Greek root of pericope means "something cut" (*koptein*) "all around" (*peri*). Therefore, a pericope is an isolated passage (a narrative scene or a piece of discourse) that can easily be cut out of the wider narrative in which it is embedded in order to be examined closely. A pericope has an identifiable beginning and end and possesses a unified topic, theme, or logic.

If we are going to interpret a single pericope, the first step in preparing the surface before digging for meaning is *establishing its boundaries*. Often the scope of a pericope is intuitively evident, but in some incidences the gospel writers have done such a good job pasting the various pericopae together into a unified narrative that it is difficult to determine where one passage ends and the next begins. We must be careful not to trust either the verse divisions (which were not added to the New Testament until 1551 C.E.) or the text divisions and headings provided by modern translators. They may or may not correspond correctly to the breaks between pericopae. Therefore, we must rely on transition indicators provided by the gospel writers themselves.

There are three types of such indicators. The first is a change in **setting**. When a new scene is introduced, the narrator will often indicate that *time* has lapsed and/or that Jesus is now in a new *location*. Sometimes both time and place changes will be present and other times only one—a pericope may begin with a change in time even though it is located in the same place as the previous scene or vice versa. To illustrate the identification of these changes in setting, let's turn to Mark 1:9–20. We have printed the text without verse or paragraph divisions so that our first approach to the text is not prejudiced. We should walk through the text, identifying every indication of time or place and analyzing whether those found represent a shift in scene.

We have marked the indicators in **bold** and commented to the right:

In those days Jesus came **from Nazareth of Galilee** and was baptized by John in the **Jordan**. And just as he was coming up out of the water, he saw the heavens torn apart and the Spirit descending like a dove on him. And a voice came from heaven, "You are my Son, the Beloved; with you I am well pleased." And the Spirit **immediately** drove him out into the **wilderness**. He was in the wilderness forty days, tempted by Satan; and he was with the wild beasts; and the angels waited on him. Now **after John was arrested**, Jesus came to **Galilee**, proclaiming the good news of God, and saying, "The time is fulfilled, and the kingdom of God has come near; repent, and believe in the good news." As Jesus passed along **the Sea of Galilee**, he saw Simon and his brother Andrew casting a net into the sea—for they were fishermen. And Jesus said to them, "Follow me and I will make you fish for people." And **immediately** they left their nets and followed him. As he **went a little farther**, he saw James son of Zebedee and his brother John, who were in their boat mending the nets. **Immediately** he called them; and they left their father Zebedee in the boat with the hired men, and followed him.

This scene opens with a time indicator ("in those days") that loosely connects this scene with the previous one (John preaching at the Jordan). The opening also describes Jesus' movement from one place (where no events are described) to another (where the scene that follows is narrated).

The use of "immediately" makes it clear that what follows is intimately connected with what precedes and does not indicate a shift, but the change in place ("Jordan" to "wilderness") indicates a new scene begins.

The time indicator sets Jesus' new action in relation to John's previous actions, and the place indicator returns Jesus to Galilee, but not necessarily Nazareth.

This place indicator specifies where in Galilee this scene takes place, whereas the previous setting was more general.

Again "immediately" marks continuity, and since there is no shift in location, there is no new pericope at this point or the next occurrence of immediately.

"Went a little farther" still keeps Jesus passing along the Sea of Galilee, so this phrase does not indicate a change in setting, but movement within the same setting.

The second indicator of a division between pericopae is a change in **characters**. Jesus is, of course, the main character in the gospels and thus present in most scenes. But the person(s) whom Jesus is observing, healing, or teaching, or with whom he is in dialogue or conflict changes rapidly. Let's consider Mark 1:9–20 again to see how this category of indicators (marked below in *italics*) appears. To see how this category complements the changes in setting we have already noted, we have made paragraph breaks at the changes of setting and left the bold print in place:

In those days *Jesus* came **from Nazareth of Galilee** and was baptized by *John* in the **Jordan**. And just as he was coming up out of the water, he saw the heavens torn apart and the *Spirit* descending like a dove on him. And a *voice came from heaven,* "You are my Son, the Beloved; with you I am well pleased."

The previous passage focused on John, but in this scene John and Jesus meet.

The Spirit is introduced, but the heavenly voice takes center stage.

And the *Spirit* **immediately** drove him out into the **wilderness**. He was in the wilderness forty days, tempted by *Satan*; and he was with the wild beasts; and the angels waited on him.

The Spirit acts again and leads Jesus to meet another character—Satan.

Now **after** *John* **was arrested**, *Jesus* came to **Galilee**, proclaiming the good news of God, and saying, "The time is fulfilled, and the kingdom of God has come near; repent, and believe in the good news."

A reference back to John (offstage) removes him from the narrative altogether. Jesus is the only character in this scene (except Jesus' implied audience).

As Jesus passed along **the Sea of Galilee**, he saw *Simon and his brother Andrew* casting a net into the sea—for they were fishermen. And Jesus said to them, "Follow me

The scene shifts from Jesus' being alone to his meeting Simon and Andrew.

and I will make you fish for people." And **immediately** they left their nets and followed him. As he **went a little farther,** he saw *James son of Zebedee and his brother John,* who were in their boat mending the nets. **Immediately** he called them; and they left their father Zebedee in the boat with the hired men, and followed him.

Although new characters are introduced, Jesus' action toward James and John is identical to his action toward Simon and Andrew. Thus, this is still part of the same scene.

The third indicator one can use to determine the beginning and/or end of a pericope is a change of ***theme***, ***topic***, or ***issue*** being addressed. This type of change can be much less obvious than the first two. Still, it is important to consider these sorts of changes, for sometimes there will be no change in setting or characters even though the text under consideration may best be understood as comprising more than one pericope. Consider, for instance, the Sermon on the Mount in Matthew 5:1–7:29. For three chapters Matthew presents Jesus as speaking without interruption. There is no change of setting or characters, but clearly this section of text is not a single pericope. Matthew has collected numerous short units of Jesus' teachings and has pasted them together into a single sermon. The basis on which they are collected together is a similarity of themes, topics, vocabulary, and so forth. But *similar* elements are not the same thing as *identical* elements. For example, the pericopae in Matthew 6:19–34 (a subsection of the Sermon on the Mount) are primarily related to the issue of material possessions. They do not, however, all approach the issue in the same way.

Let us consider again our example from Mark 1:9–20. Topic and theme indicators are underlined.

In those days *Jesus* came **from Nazareth of Galilee** and was <u>bap-tized</u> by *John* in the **Jordan**. And just as he was coming up out of the water, he saw the heavens torn

<u>This scene is an epiphany in which Jesus, through his baptism, is anointed as God's Son.</u>

apart and the *Spirit* descending like a dove on him. And a *voice came from heaven,* "You are my Son, the Beloved; with you I am well pleased."

And the *Spirit* **immediately** drove him out into the **wilderness**. He was in the wilderness forty days, tempted by *Satan*; and he was with the wild beasts; and the angels waited on him.

> God's claiming Jesus as God's Son is followed by a seemingly opposite theme—conflict with Satan.

Now **after *John* was arrested,** *Jesus* came to **Galilee**, proclaiming the good news of God, and saying, "The time is fulfilled, and the kingdom of God has come near; repent, and believe in the good news."

> Jesus' victory over Satan is implied as the scene shifts to a summary of the content of Jesus' preaching.

As Jesus passed along **the Sea of Galilee**, he saw *Simon and his brother Andrew* casting a net into the sea—for they were fishermen. And Jesus said to them, "Follow me and I will make you fish for people." And **immediately** they left their nets and followed him. As he **went a little farther,** he saw *James son of Zebedee and his brother John,* who were in their boat mending the nets. **Immediately** he called them; and they left their father Zebedee in the boat with the hired men, and followed him.

> Having summarized Jesus' preaching, the narrator shifts to focus on the calling of Jesus' first disciples.

Unlike Mark 1:9–20, not every scene change in the synoptic gospels is accompanied by setting, character, and theme indicators. Thus, it is important always to examine all three in establishing the boundaries of a pericope.

Establishing the Text

Once we have established the pericope, we are ready to turn our attention to the *text* of the passage itself. We do not have autographed copies of the gospels. In other words, no original manuscripts of Matthew, Mark, or Luke exist. Since there was no printing press in the first centuries of the Common Era, professional scribes had the task of copying books by hand for publication. This method, of course, leaves much room for human error. Moreover, when these books first began to be circulated among first-century Christian communities, they were valued but were not yet honored as canonical scripture. Thus, scribes felt free to make changes in the texts they were copying. They might clean up the style, clarify the meaning of an ambiguous sentence, harmonize one gospel account of an event with that found in another gospel, or even change something in the text they didn't like. Usually the changes were minor rewordings, but some copies of the gospels include major omissions or additions.

The fact that the first typeset copy of the Bible did not appear until the mid-fifteenth century means that for more than fourteen centuries scribes were copying the gospels by hand, making numerous mistakes and at times changing the text intentionally (intentional alterations happened much more rarely after the gospels were canonized). And, indeed, they were copying copies that already contained errors and changes. And the copies they were copying were made from copies that contained errors and changes. And so on and so forth. The result is that we have more than 5,300 Greek manuscripts of the New Testament (or parts of it) with tens of thousands of *textual variants*—disagreements among manuscripts concerning wording, inclusion of pericopae, and so forth. Biblical scholars must compare and contrast these variants as they attempt to make educated guesses concerning the original wording of the text. This process of discerning the original script is called ***text criticism***.

The scholars who translated the New Testament for the NRSV have already done this work for their English readers.

We are never even aware of most of the textual choices they make on our behalf because the choices are so clear-cut that they need no comment—most mistakes made by scribes are blatant errors. Nevertheless, textual variants that seem to be the result of intentional changes do not always have clear-cut solutions. When two or more variants seem plausible as original wording, the NRSV translators describe the alternative to their choice in a footnote. At this point, we have to accept the choice made by the translators or opt for the alternate reading. We should be careful not to choose the reading we *like* the best, but the one we believe to be closest to the original. These are difficult choices to make, especially for English readers, because we are not (and cannot be) fully informed. But English readers are not completely at the mercy of the NRSV translators. There are two things we can and should do.

The first thing we do when considering such textual variants is to try to imagine *why* a scribe changed the text. We must assume that the scribe was trying to *improve* the text. This rationale means that the more problematic variant should usually be considered the more original reading. A major example involves the ending to Mark. Several families of manuscripts have very different endings to this gospel. The versions agree through 16:1– 8. In the first seven verses of this pericope, the women who come to anoint Jesus' body find the tomb empty, are told of Jesus' resurrection, and are instructed to go tell his disciples to meet Jesus in Galilee. Then verse 8 reads,

> So they went out and fled from the tomb, for terror and amazement had seized them; and they said nothing to anyone, for they were afraid.

Some manuscripts end here while others continue, narrating appearances of the risen Jesus. When considering whether we think the text originally ended at 16:8 or continued, we must ask of each variant, Why would a scribe have added or omitted this? It is easy to see why scribes would have found the ending at verse 8 problematic. If Mark ends at 16:8, it means that this gospel has no resurrection appearances like the other gospels and, even more importantly, ends with a tone of despair as the women's fear gets in the way of the disciples' learning of Jesus' resurrection and meeting him in Galilee. Thus, the rationale that the more problematic variant is usually the more original reading would lead us to argue that the gospel of Mark originally ended at 16:8, and the other endings were later additions. And, indeed, most New Testament scholars agree that Mark's original ending was 16:8. On the other hand, the rule of accepting the most difficult reading as the most original can be overemphasized. In some instances, the more difficult variant might have been made by a scribe who misunderstood the pericope.

The second thing we do when considering textual variants is to compare how different translations handle the textual issue. This step will help us test our hypothesis concerning why a scribe would have added, omitted, or changed a piece of text. If most translations we check agree with the choice of the NRSV, then we can feel comfortable following that choice. If they do not, we must rely more heavily on our own hypothesis.

A final step is needed in establishing our text. It is important that English interpreters keep themselves aware of the fact that they are reading a translation. Not only have translators made many choices for us concerning problems with the Greek manuscripts, they have also made many choices concerning problems with the Greek language. The act of translation is not a mathematical process in which *this Greek word = that English word.* Word order is used differently in the two languages to make emphasis. Many words have several possible nuances or even radically different meanings depending on how they are used. And some words in one language do not have an equivalent in the other. For instance, in Greek there is a verb form of *faith.* The English translator must choose whether to translate this verb as *believe* or *trust* but knows that neither really matches the Greek meaning perfectly. All this is to say that translation itself is a form of interpretation, and before moving ahead with our exegesis we need to **establish the translation** we will use.

We have chosen to use the NRSV as our primary translation, but our loyalty is to the gospel we are interpreting, not to the translation we are reading. Therefore, we may need to adjust the English vocabulary at points in the pericope. The NRSV itself provides the starting point for evaluating the translation. The translators note when there is ambiguity of which they feel English readers should be aware. We should also compare the NRSV with other English translations. If we find that other translations agree with each other against the NRSV or use language that flows better or makes better sense, we may need to substitute wording for part of our pericope. More than looking for slight linguistic variations, we want to note only those differences between translations that change the sense of a sentence or pericope in a significant way. In other words, style is not the issue; meaning is.

Establishing the Plain Sense

Once the pericope's boundaries have been defined, and the text and translation have been chosen, only one surface issue remains before we move deeper in our interpretation. It is important to understand fully ***the plain sense*** of the pericope. Do I understand every single thing that is happening or is said in this passage? What is dropsy? Is Caesarea a city, a region, or a country? How much is a denarius? Before attempting to understand the *significance* of a pericope, one must be sure to understand (at the surface level) all the vocabulary and references in the pericope. To do this, interpreters simply need to look up any ambiguous elements of the content in a dictionary, encyclopedia, or Bible dictionary.

Once the pericope, the text, and the plain sense have all been established, the interpreter is ready to dig deeper into the text. Let's examine how these preparatory steps work on an example pericope.

Example: Matthew 12:46–50

Establishing the Pericope

We begin by determining the limits of our passage. Does the pericope begin at verse 46 and end at verse 50 as we have designated, or does it need to be expanded or shortened? Backing up to 12:38, we find scribes and Pharisees addressing Jesus, and he begins his response in verse 39. Jesus continues in direct speech through verse 45. In verse 46, the narrator speaks again (for the first time since verse 38):

> While he was still speaking to the crowds, his mother and his brothers were standing outside, wanting to speak to him.

The introductory phrase in this sentence ("while he was still speaking") indicates that there has been no change of setting. The event that is about to be described happens in the same place and time as that which has just been described. The phrase "his mother and brothers," however, does introduce new characters. The focus is no longer on the crowd (i.e., the scribes and Pharisees), but on Jesus' family. Thus, a new pericope does indeed begin at verse 46.

In verse 47 "someone" tells Jesus his family is present. Jesus' response to this news begins in verse 48 and ends in verse 50. Then in 13:1 the narrator states,

> That same day Jesus went out of the house and sat beside the sea.

This sentence begins with a time referent ("That same day") that emphasizes both continuity and discontinuity with that which preceded. The implication of the phrase is that what follows is set on the *same* day as (continuity) but at a *later* time than (discontinuity) the dialogue with the scribes and Pharisees and the discussion concerning Jesus' family. In addition to this change in time, a change in place is indicated by the movement of Jesus. He moves from "the house" to "the sea." The change of setting marked by a change of both time and place indicates that verse 50 is the end of the pericope. Therefore, the full pericope we will investigate is Matthew 12:46–50.

This delineation of the boundaries is confirmed by noting the shift in themes/topics. In 12:38–45 the text deals with the request for a sign from Jesus. In 13:1ff. Jesus begins teaching the crowds by using various parables. Our pericope deals with Jesus' family.

Establishing the Text

Now that we have determined the limits of our pericope, we must establish the text itself, which includes issues related to both manuscript transmission and translation from Greek into English. Our starting point for doing this is any footnotes offered by the NRSV. There are two in this passage. The first is in verse 47, which reads,

> Someone told him, "Look, your mother and your brothers are
> standing outside, wanting to speak to you."

The NRSV footnote at the end of this verse says, "Other ancient authorities lack verse 47." This means either that some scribes deleted this sentence from the pericope or that some added it to the pericope. The NRSV translators' decision to include the sentence shows that they think some scribes deleted it, and thus the original text included the verse. The fact that they noted that the sentence is missing from some manuscripts, however, means that there is significant evidence for the other choice. We turn to other translations to test the NRSV's decision. Although not all translations are worthy of consideration in an exegetical endeavor, numerous ones could be helpful in this step. The simplest way to compare translations is to check the verse in a parallel Bible. One published by Oxford Press (*The Complete Parallel Bible*, New York: Oxford Press, 1993) contains the *New Revised Standard Version* (translated by an ecumenical team of scholars in the United States), the *Revised English Bible* (translated by an ecumenical team of scholars in Great Britain), the *New American Bible* (translated by a team of Catholic scholars in the United States), and the *New Jerusalem Bible* (translated by a team of Catholic scholars in Great Britain). What we find in these other translations is a curious situation:

NRSV

[46]While he was still speaking to the crowds, his mother and his brothers were standing outside, wanting to speak to him. [47]Someone told him, "Look, your mother and your brothers are standing outside, wanting to speak to you."[r] [48]But to the one who had told him this, Jesus[s] replied, "Who is my mother, and who are my brothers?" [49]And pointing to his disciples, he said, "Here are my mother and my brothers! [50]For whoever does the will of my Father in heaven is my brother and sister and mother."

[r]Other ancient authorities lack verse 47
[s]Gk *he*

NAB

[46]While he was still speaking to the crowds, his mother and his brothers appeared outside, wishing to speak with him. [[47]Someone told him, "your mother and your brothers are standing outside, asking to speak with you."] [48]But he said in reply to the one who told him, "Who is my mother? Who are my brothers?" [49]And stretching out his hand toward his disciples, he said, "Here are my mother and my brothers. [50]For whoever does the will of my heavenly Father is my brother, and sister, and mother."

12,47: This verse is omitted in some important textual witnesses, including Codex Sinaiticus (original reading) and Codex Vaticanus.

REB

[46]He was still speaking to the crowd when his mother and brothers appeared; they stood outside, wanting to speak to him. [47]Someone said, 'Your mother and your brothers are standing outside; they want to speak to you.' [48]Jesus turned to the man who brought the message, and said, 'Who is my mother? Who are my brothers?' [49]and pointing to his disciples, he said, 'Here are my mother and my brothers. [50]Whoever does the will of my heavenly Father is my brother and sister and mother.'

NJB

[46]He was still speaking to the crowds when suddenly his mother and his brothers[n] were standing outside and were anxious to have a word with him. [47][o] [48]But to the man who told him this Jesus replied, 'Who is my mother? Who are my brothers?' [49]And stretching out his hand towards his disciples he said, 'Here are my mother and my brothers. Anyone who does the will of my Father in heaven is my brother and sister and mother.'

[n]**12** Not necessarily Mary's children. The Hebr. And Aram. Word includes cousins and close relations. [o]**12** v.47 ('Someone said to him: Your mother and your brothers are standing outside and want to speak to you') is omitted by some important textual witnesses. It is probably a restatement of v.46 modelled on Mk and Lk.

The REB includes verse 47 without note. Thus, these translators have a higher level of confidence that verse 47 was originally part of Matthew's text than do the NRSV translators. (If we had been reading the REB without comparing other translations, we would not even have known that a textual problem existed at this point in the pericope.)

The NAB includes the verse in the text but encloses it in brackets and notes that some manuscripts (including the one they consider to be the "original reading") do not include this verse. This translation, therefore, exhibits a very low degree of certainty that the verse might have been part of the original text.

Finally, the NJB includes only the verse number "47" in the text in brackets, and in the footnotes argues that the sentence was an addition by a scribe who was harmonizing Matthew to Mark and Luke. Thus, the translators strongly assert that verse 47 should probably not be included in the text.

Often translations agree and give English readers a strong sense of certainty in the choice made concerning a textual problem. The lack of agreement among the four translations just considered, however, does little to settle conclusively the issue concerning the inclusion of verse 47 in our pericope. We can, at least, take comfort in the fact that we are in no worse a situation than the experts. But how do we proceed from here? Two of the translations provide rationales for the choices they made. If we evaluate them, we will be better equipped to decide whether the verse should be considered part of the original text or not.

The NAB cites the importance of specific manuscripts in choosing to include the verse in brackets. Since we nonspecialists are unable to evaluate the manuscript evidence, this rationale is of little help to us. (Throckmorton's *Gospel Parallels* does offer a description of the various important manuscripts and manuscript types, but they are still difficult for a nonspecialist to sift through.)

The NJB asserts that verse 47 is a scribal addition meant to make Matthew's version look more like Mark's and Luke's versions. While this conjecture may be correct, it is also possible that the author of the gospel of Matthew himself included the sentence since he was using Mark as his source (see Excursus 1). If we use a synopsis to compare Matthew's version of this sentence with Mark's (for more on comparison of gospels using a synopsis, see chapter 5), we find:

MATTHEW	MARK
	[32]A crowd was sitting
[47]Someone told him,	around him; and they said
"Look, your mother and	to him, "Your mother and
your brothers are standing	your brothers and sisters
outside, wanting to speak	are outside asking for
to you."	you." (3:32)

Although the meaning of the two sentences is pretty much the same, there is a significant difference. In Mark, the character speaking to Jesus is "the crowd" (a group). In Matthew, the speaker is "someone" (a single person). If we read forward in Matthew, we find that the narrator begins the next sentence with the phrase, "But to *the one* who had told him this..." (v. 48). This phrasing can be read as necessitating the antecedent "*Someone* told him..." If verse 47 were an addition, we might expect similar textual problems with verse 48. Since none of the translations note such a textual problem with this phrase in verse 48, we are on solid ground conjecturing (although we cannot be certain) that verse 47 was part of the original text. (The nice thing about this particular textual problem is that neither the inclusion nor exclusion of verse 47 radically alters the meaning of the pericope. This is not always the case. Some textual problems cause serious interpretation problems.)

The second footnote in the NRSV that we must consider as we establish our text is found in verse 48. The word *Jesus* is marked, and the note reads, "Gk *he.*" This means that the translators have substituted *Jesus* for the pronoun *he* to make unambiguous who is speaking. This is a common practice of the NRSV, does not change the meaning of the text, and requires no investigation.

Still left to explore, however, is a comparison of the English translations of the pericope in order to establish our ***translation***.

If we use the same four translations (since our parallel Bible is still open), we find numerous minor differences among them.

> For example, whereas in verse 46 the NRSV reads, "his mother and brothers were standing outside" the NJB has "*suddenly*...were standing outside." Later in the same verse the NJB has "*anxious* to have a word with him" instead of "*wanting* to speak to him" (NRSV).
>
> And in verse 47 the NAB says the family was "*asking* to speak" to Jesus, while the NRSV reads "*wanting* to speak" to him. These examples of differences in wording make only a little difference in the meaning of the pericope. The NJB's use of "suddenly" and "anxious" in the opening sentence of the passage raises the level of intensity in the scene a slight bit over that in the NRSV. And the NAB's choice of "asking" (an action) implies a slightly more active role on the part of Jesus' family than is present in the NRSV's "wanting" (an internal desire).
>
> In verse 49, the NAB and the NJB present Jesus as "*stretching* out his hand toward his disciples" instead of "pointing" to them (NRSV and REB). As English readers, we may guess that this difference may be nothing more than a more literal or more formal translation of the Greek, which the NRSV correctly translates into the more common English idiom. On the other hand, we might wonder whether the stretching forth of Jesus' hand is more ritualistic in nature than simply pointing. Does the gesture indicate that Jesus is pronouncing some form of blessing? Again, this case is difficult for English readers to decide. Since Jesus is replying to the person who told him of his family's presence and not to the disciples directly, the gesture is more likely one of directing the hearer's attention than it is ritualistic. Thus, we will maintain the NRSV wording. However, we should keep the NAB and NJB translation in mind, in case later exegetical steps lead us to reconsider the physical action that accompanies Jesus' words.

Having established the boundaries, the text, and the translation, we can now assert that the pericope we will be interpreting is Matthew 12:46–50, which reads:

> [46]While he was still speaking to the crowds, his mother and his brothers were standing outside, wanting to speak to him.

⁴⁷Someone told him, "Look, your mother and your brothers are standing outside, wanting to speak to you." ⁴⁸But to the one who had told him this, Jesus replied, "Who is my mother, and who are my brothers?" ⁴⁹And pointing to his disciples, he said, "Here are my mother and my brothers! ⁵⁰For whoever does the will of my Father in heaven is my brother and sister and mother."

Establishing the Plain Sense

Our final step in preparing the surface for deeper interpretation is to establish the literal sense of the pericope. At first reading, there appear to be no unfamiliar or ambivalent terms or references. However, while we were comparing translations, we should have noticed a footnote in the NJB's version of verse 46. At the word *brothers* this translation comments,

> Not necessarily Mary's children. The Hebrew and Aramaic word includes cousins and close relations.

The question for the interpreter, therefore, is whether the characters in the story are Jesus' immediate family or his extended family. At this point, we are not concerned with the historical question of the makeup of Jesus' immediate family; we are only concerned with the plain sense of the passage. Simple reasoning can help here. First, we have claimed that Matthew was written in Greek, not Hebrew or Aramaic. Thus, the NJB's claim is based on a conjecture about the original words of Jesus (which probably were Aramaic), not Matthew's version of the scene. Second, the comment reveals a Catholic doctrinal bias concerning Mary's perpetual virginity being projected onto the pericope. If we look up "Mary, the Virgin" in *HarperCollins Bible Dictionary* (p. 658), we find that the author who writes the entry assumes that Mary had other sons besides Jesus. Therefore, the plain sense of the text would seem to be that Mary and her *sons* have come to speak to Jesus.

We have finished preparing the text to be interpreted. We have established the pericope as Matthew 12:46–50. We have established the text as including verse 47. We have chosen to accept the NRSV translation as it stands. And we understand the plain sense of the pericope. We are now ready to move to the next step in our interpretive process: exploring the socio-historical background of the passage.

For Further Reading

Epp, Eldon Jay. "Textual Criticism." In *The New Testament and Its Modern Interpreters*, ed. E. J. Epp and G. W. MacRae, 75–126. Atlanta: Scholars Press, 1989.

Hayes, John H., and Carl R. Holladay. "Textual Criticism: The Quest for the Original Wording." In *Biblical Exegesis: A Beginner's Handbook*, rev. ed., 33–44. Atlanta: John Knox Press, 1987.

―――――. "Grammatical Criticism: The Language of the Text." In *Biblical Exegesis: A Beginner's Handbook*, rev. ed., 59–72. Atlanta: John Knox Press, 1987.

Metzger, Bruce M. Introduction to *Textual Commentary on the Greek New Testament*. 2d ed. xiii–xxxi. New York: United Bible Societies, 1995.

> While this commentary is directed toward Greek readers, the introductory material describes the history of the transmission of the New Testament and the criteria used for making textual decisions in a way that may be helpful.

Throckmorton, Burton H., Jr. "Preface to the Fifth Edition." In *Gospel Parallels*, ix–xxii. Nashville: Thomas Nelson, 1992.

> Throckmorton describes the various manuscripts scholars use to perform text criticism on the New Testament. This discussion provides a great deal of information in a small amount of space.

EXCURSUS 1

Development of the Synoptic Gospels

It is not possible, in a work of this length, to offer a detailed argument for a particular hypothesis concerning the process by which the synoptic gospels developed. But it is important to at least summarize the understanding of the movement from Jesus of Nazareth to the gospels of Matthew, Mark, and Luke that underlies the development of most of the exegetical methods described in this book.

The process begins with the *Jesus movement* itself. Although our historical knowledge of Jesus of Nazareth is limited, it is clear that a group of people who were attracted to his teachings gathered around him as his disciples/students. Teachings and events that made an especially strong impression on these disciples would have been remembered and passed on after his death.

One of the great challenges to New Testament scholarship is answering the historical question of what happened next. We know the result, but not the process. The result was that the attraction to Jesus' teachings evolved into worship of Jesus as the Christ. The Jesus movement became the Christian movement. In other words, somehow the preaching *of* Jesus was replaced by preaching *about* Jesus. So thorough was this process that our earliest New Testament writings (the letters of Paul) rarely even mention the teachings or ministry of Jesus at all. Instead, the letters focus on the death of Jesus the Christ. So the next step in the development of the gospel traditions was ***the preaching of Jesus' crucifixion and resurrection***. Therefore, the oral shape of ***the passion narrative*** is most likely the oldest part of the gospels and took written form before other parts.

As the preaching about the death and resurrection spread and time passed, interest arose in Jesus' teachings and in the events of his ministry. ***Oral traditions*** arose that told of miracles performed by Jesus, parables he taught, and confrontations he had with religious authorities. These traditions, used for the purposes of proclamation, were ***collected*** and eventually ***written down***.

Most New Testament scholars agree that ***Mark*** is the earliest written gospel (at least, that is still extant). Around the year 70 C.E. (when the Jerusalem temple was destroyed) "Mark" (the attribution of authorship of the gospels is not original, but names of the gospels continue to be used for the authors for the sake of convenience) collected individual traditions about Jesus' ministry in Galilee along with the passion narrative set in Jerusalem and pasted them together into a theological narrative that began with Jesus' baptism and ended at his empty tomb.

Most scholars also agree that ***Matthew*** and ***Luke*** were written independently of each other ten to twenty years after Mark was written. Both "Matthew" and "Luke" (again, the true authors of the gospels are unknown) used the gospel of Mark as one of their primary sources, following its outline to a great degree, but expanding its content significantly. While there are significant narrative additions in both gospels (e.g., the birth and resurrection narratives), the majority of the material that Matthew and Luke add to Mark is speech material. Many of these sayings are found in both Matthew and Luke. And many times Matthew and Luke use exactly the same wording in their presentations of these sayings. The simplest explanation for this phenomenon would be that either Matthew copied these sayings from Luke's gospel or Luke used Matthew's gospel as a sources, except for the fact that Matthew and Luke nearly always insert these sayings into different places in Mark's narrative outline. For example, Jesus' lament over Jerusalem is presented in both Mathew and Luke in nearly word-for-word parallelism. But Matthew inserts the saying into Mark's temple dialogue just before Jesus is arrested (23:37–39), whereas Luke inserts the pericope into a travel narrative created to present Jesus' teaching on his way from Galilee to Jerusalem (13:34–35). If Matthew had used Luke as a source or vice versa, one would expect to find significant amounts of both parallel wording and parallel placement. Because so little parallel placement exists, scholars looked for an answer that would explain the parallel wording and differing placement. The hypothesis most scholars hold is that Matthew and Luke had a second major source in addition to Mark. Scholars call this sayings source (or collection of shared written sources) "Q," from the German word *quelle* which means "source."

But Matthew and Luke also contain material unique to each of their gospels. Some of these sayings and stories may be "Q" material that one or the other gospel writer chose not to include. But some of it must come from other sources as well. Thus, scholars label the materials unique to Matthew with the letter "M" and those unique to Luke, "L." In graphic presentation, the final stages of the process by which the synoptic gospels developed would look like the following:

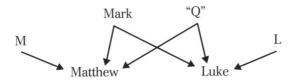

CHAPTER 2

Social and
Historical Background

All biblical texts are historical, but they are not necessarily history. When we are referring specifically to the gospels, claiming that they are historical means two things. First, it means that they are *historically bound*. The gospels were not spoken by God in a vacuous heaven separated from the ebb and flow of earthly existence. They were written by Christians who were trying faithfully to tell the story of the Christ event in such a way that it would have a positive effect on the perceptions, emotions, theology, and lives of their audience. Like all humans, these authors were creatures of context. They were defined by the culture and period in which they lived. Their worldviews were intimately bound to the cosmopolitan, pluralistic, hellenized, imperial, patriarchal, agrarian, oral, Mediterranean world of the Roman Empire. And so are their gospels. The second thing we mean when we say that the gospels are historical is that they *contain history*. They focus on a historical person, Jesus of Nazareth. And as Luke says in his prologue, some of the accounts of events included in the gospels were passed down by eyewitnesses (1:2). By tying these accounts back to the earliest sources, Luke implies that they are historically accurate.

The fact that the gospels are historically bound and contain historical elements, however, should not lead us to confuse them with history books. Their goal is to preach the gospel, not to publish a journalistic report (thus the difference between the *good news* and a *newspaper*). Even as he claims the historicity of his sources, Luke states that his primary intent is to write an orderly narrative so that Christian readers "may know the truth concerning the things about which you have been instructed" (1:4). The purpose of the gospels is to proclaim truth of an ultimate, not a historical, nature. Put in its classic, theological formulation, the gospels proclaim the story of the Jesus Christ of faith; they do not narrate the biography of the Jesus of Nazareth of history.

The Interpreter's Approach to the Historical Text

It is not the goal of this book to argue, one way or another, whether in the synoptic gospels the historical picture of Jesus and the proclamatory picture of Christ are identical or diverge widely. We simply make the distinction between the goal of writing history and that of writing religious narrative in order to focus the *interpreter's* goal in relation to the historical character of the gospels. If readers turn to the gospels as religious stories to which they grant the authority to shape, confirm, or transform their views of self, world, and God, they should not get bogged down trying to use the narratives to answer historical questions. To do so is to fail to explore the text on its own terms.

Nevertheless, at least an elementary understanding of the sociohistorical world of the text is required if the interpreter is to uncover and come to understand fully the layers of religious and theological meaning a pericope conveys to its readers. A two-thousand-year gap lies between modern readers and the world of the gospels, and the interpreter must be historically sensitive so as to avoid (eisegetically) forcing modern values, views of the universe, or perceptions of daily lifestyles upon the ancient text. The gospels and their pericopae must be appreciated as expressions of the ancient world, which they reflect and in which they arose.

The first step in such appreciation is the ***identification*** of elements in the pericope that require location within ancient history and culture. There are more of these elements than we might think at first. Most obvious are *references* to historical events and persons, ancient practices, rituals, and daily living conditions (food, clothes, shelter, work), and ancient geographical sites. More subtle are latent *values* in the text that are culturally defined—views concerning relationships, class, gender, ethnic identity, personality, the physical world, political existence, and ethics.

At first glance, these things may seem identical or at least analogous to modern values, but ***investigation*** will show that the differences may be significant. They are not spelled out in the text because the gospel writers assume that the references are understood or that the values are shared by their first-century audiences. Since the references are foreign to us, however, we must investigate them in order to understand the text's significance in its original context. Such investigation is the second step in dealing with the social and historical elements in a pericope. For beginning interpreters, investigation of these elements can be difficult. We are unable to visit archaeological digs in the Holy Land, read reams of classical Greek literature, or study ancient Mediterranean political and social history in great depth. Therefore, we must rely on the research of scholars in these fields. The problem with such reliance is that there are hundreds of volumes of research on the relationship between the Bible and the context in which it was originally shaped and read.

There are two types of works that will have condensed pertinent social and historical information for us as we approach a particular pericope. The first type is a *commentary*. Commentaries, which analyze gospels pericope by pericope, will discuss social and historical data that the commentator considers relevant. The problem with consulting a commentary at this early point in the interpretive process is that it could prejudice our interpretation of our pericope. Commentaries should be used as dialogue partners. We use them to test (and therefore, expand or alter) our interpretation by comparing it with another reader's interpretation, not to serve as an interpretation from which our own interpretation proceeds. Therefore, we do better to delay our consultation of commentaries until later in the interpretive process and instead turn to the second type of work that condenses historical and social information into an accessible format: the *Bible dictionary*. By using a Bible dictionary to investigate those elements in our pericope that we have identified as needful of location in their original setting, we are able to gain an elementary understanding of the social, psychological, political, and economic nuances of our text and will have a better sense of the kind of impact its context would have had on a first-century audience.

Once all the social and historical elements of the pericope have been identified and investigated at an elementary level, the interpreter will be ready to move to the next step of interpretation. Before moving to that next step, let's examine how this step works on our example pericope.

Example: Matthew 12:46–50

Identification of Sociohistorical Elements

This pericope raises several historical questions concerning Jesus' family. Where is Jesus' father? How many siblings did Jesus have? Why are his sisters not mentioned anywhere else in the New Testament? If we were researching the historical Jesus and using this pericope as one of our sources, these would be interesting questions to pursue. But if we are striving to discover and interpret the various layers of meaning in the pericope, such historical questions sidetrack our efforts.

We need to focus only on the types of social and historical questions that will help us understand the passage better. Whereas we are not concerned with the specific historical details of Jesus' family, we should be concerned about the views and values that first-century Mediterranean culture placed on the *family* unit. How did the family function, and how was it viewed in the time in which Matthew was written?

Another element that may be better understood by examination in its sociohistorical setting is the portrayal of the *disciples*. Discipleship language is so common within modern Christian discourse that we may too readily assume that we know what the gospel means when it speaks of Jesus' disciples. We must be careful not to project our use of discipleship language (as well as our acceptance of the presentation of the disciples in sermons and popular devotional materials) onto Matthew's presentation of the disciples in his sociohistorical context.

Investigation of Sociohistorical Elements

If we look up *family* in the *HarperCollins Bible Dictionary* (p. 330), we find a full-page article that discusses the nuclear and extended families and the clan and tribe in ancient Israel. Although this information relates to a period earlier than that of the first century C.E., it is not completely irrelevant. The section on the nuclear family at least provides a historical and social framework in which to consider the dynamics present in the pericope when Jesus aligns himself with a new familial group:

> **The Nuclear Family:** The smallest family unit was the nuclear family (the "house"), which usually occupied its own dwelling. The nuclear family normally consisted of parents and their unmarried children, although occasionally non-kin such as slaves or long-term visitors also shared the family's living quarters. Archaeological evidence suggests that no more than six or seven people occupied the average house on a regular basis. Within the nuclear family children were socialized by being taught the customs and lore of their people (Prov. 1:8; 6:20), including the story of God's dealings with Israel (Exod. 10:2; 12:26; 13:8; Deut. 4:9; 6:7, 20–25; 32:7, 46). Well into the monarchical period (ca. 1020–586 B.C.), each nuclear family was also a self-sustaining economic unit. Agricultural products grown by the family were stored in the house, and any animals that the family might own were quartered there. Living arrangements may have been different in the period before Israel's settlement in Canaan (thirteenth–twelfth centuries B.C.), but there is little firm evidence on this point.

Most of the authority in the nuclear family belonged to the father, who exercised legal control over his children and wife, although his power was not absolute (Exod. 21:7–11; Deut. 21:15–21). Children were expected to honor and obey their parents, and failure to do so was a serious matter (Exod. 20:12; 21:15, 17; Lev. 20:9; Deut. 27:16; Prov. 30:17). The integrity of the family was further protected by harsh laws against adultery and incest (Exod. 20:14; Lev. 18:20; 20:10–21; Deut. 5:18; 22:22). However, families could be dissolved through divorce (Deut. 24:1–4).

Children remained under their father's control until they were married, when they left home to start a new family unit. Marriages were carefully regulated (Lev. 18). In early Israel polygyny was common (Gen. 4:19; 16:1–2; 22:20–24; 25:1, 6; 29:15–30), although by monarchical times this practice was limited primarily to the royal family. Even after marriage children were expected to honor their parents and were exhorted to care for them in their old age (Prov. 23:22). (Harper Collins Bible Dictionary, p. 330)

Many of the details in this essay are of no help to us as we interpret our New Testament passage because they refer to pre–New Testament times, but some important pieces of information are provided. Because Jesus was not married, he would still have been considered part of his family of origin under his father's authority. Thus, the absence of the father from the scene is striking, especially in the light of the fact that Jesus' last word identifies his family as those disciples who do the will of his "*Father* in heaven." Has Jesus substituted one Father for another and thus also substituted one family for another? Is there a relationship between the authority under which one ultimately lives and the person(s) to whom one relates most intimately? Is Jesus rejecting the *persons* of his family or the *cultural mores* of honoring his mother and remaining a legal and economic part of his original household? These issues, which would have been immediately evident to a first-century reader, would have been missed by us if we had been satisfied with thinking of Jesus' family in modern terms.

The Bible dictionary essay closes with a paragraph dealing specifically with the New Testament's presentation of the family:

> **In the NT:** NT views of the family are somewhat different from those found in the OT. On the one hand, some of Jesus' sayings subordinate family loyalty to the gospel (Matt. 10:34–39; 12:46–50; Mark 3:31–35; Luke 12:49–53). On the other hand, Jesus quoted approvingly the command to honor parents and thus supported the traditional Jewish family structure (Matt. 19:16–22; Luke 18:18–30). In the early church support of one's family was seen as a virtue (1 Tim. 5:8), but the traditional view of family was transformed by seeing the Christian community as a new family (Gal. 6:10; Eph. 2:19). (p. 330)

This statement confirms the direction of our questions concerning the tension between social expectations of loyalty to family and Jesus' statement concerning his new family (i.e., the disciples who do the will of his Father in heaven). Moreover, it shows that while our pericope focuses directly on Jesus' family, the issue underlying the passage may have more to do with a tension felt by members of the early church as they struggled with allegiance to family (which is a virtue) and to the Christian community (which is described as a new family).

Therefore, by reading the Bible dictionary article on the family, the backdrop against which we view Matthew 12:46–50 has come into much sharper focus. Matthew is not only telling a story about Jesus' defining *his* "true" family, he is telling a story that reflects and addresses a struggle of first-century Christians concerning adhering to cultural mores versus becoming part of a radically new social order that may go against those mores.

Next, we need to look up *disciples* in our Bible dictionary. We find a much shorter entry than we did for family:

> **Disciple** (translates the Gk. for "learner"), an apprentice or pupil attached to a teacher or movement; one whose allegiance is to the instruction and commitments of the teacher or movement. Closely paralleling rabbinic custom, most NT

references to "disciple" designate "followers" of Jesus, often a large group including both his closest associates (the Twelve) and a larger number who followed with varying positive response (Luke 6:17). For disciples of other persons, see Luke 11:1 and John 1:35 (John the Baptist), Matt. 22:16 and Mark 2:18 (Pharisees), John 9:28 (Moses), and Acts 6:1–7 (Christians); cf. also Isa. 8:16 (Isaiah). (p. 242)

In spite of its brevity, we do learn some important information from this paragraph. Many people and groups had disciples. In an ancient context, then, discipleship language was not just Christian language. The term *disciple* might have been as common in Matthew's day as *student* is in ours.

Usually students are defined by their relation to their teacher. But in our pericope, disciples are related to Jesus (as family) only by doing the will of the Father in heaven. Matthew, therefore, presents Jesus as stretching the understanding of discipleship common in his day. By understanding a little more of the etymology and historical use of this word we have been able to recognize a nuance in Matthew 12:46–50 we might have missed otherwise. In this pericope, Jesus is not only redefining familial ties, he is redefining discipleship. A disciple is one who shares Jesus' loyalty to the Father, not just one who is loyal to Jesus.

We have not investigated this pericope's historical and social context for the sake of the context itself. We have done so in order to be better equipped to understand what we discover as we dig into the passage. If we have done our job well, we move to the next step with both more information and more questions (better informed questions) than we had before this step.

For Further Reading

Elliott, John H. *What Is Social-Scientific Criticism?* Guides to Biblical Scholarship. Minneapolis: Fortress Press, 1993.

Garrett, Susan R. "Sociology of Early Christianity." In *Anchor Bible Dictionary*, ed. David Noel Freedman, 6.89–99. New York: Doubleday, 1992.

Hayes, John H., and Carl R. Holladay. "Historical Criticism: The Setting in Time and Space." In *Biblical Exegesis: A Beginner's Handbook,* rev. ed., 45–58. Atlanta: John Knox Press, 1987.

Malina, Bruce J. "The Social Sciences and Biblical Interpretation." In *Interpretation* 36 (1982): 229–42.

————, and Richard L. Rohrbaugh. *Social-Science Commentary on the Synoptic Gospels.* Minneapolis: Fortress Press, 1992.

Martin, Dale B. "Social-Scientific Criticism." In *To Each Its Own Meaning: An Introduction to Biblical Criticisms and Their Application,* 1st ed., ed. Steven L. McKenzie and Stephen R. Haynes 103–19. Louisville, Ky.: Westminster/John Knox Press, 1993.

Osiek, Carolyn. *What Are They Saying about the Social Setting of the New Testament?* New York: Paulist Press, 1984.

Rhoades, David. "Social Criticism: Crossing Boundaries." In *Mark & Method: New Approaches in Biblical Studies,* ed. Janice Capel Anderson and Stephen D. Moore, 135–61. Minneapolis: Fortress Press, 1992.

Stambaugh, John, and David Balch. *The New Testament in Its Social Environment.* Library of Early Christianity 2. Philadelphia: Westminster Press, 1978.

Tiffany, Frederick C., and Sharon H. Ringe. "Reading Contextually: Locating the Social Context." In *Biblical Interpretation: A Roadmap*, 95–108. Nashville: Abingdon Press, 1996.

CHAPTER 3

Literary Background

In the last chapter, we examined the importance of obtaining an elementary knowledge of the sociohistorical background of a pericope. There is, however, more to the backdrop that sets the stage for the gospels than the economic, political, psychological, social, and historical dimensions of ancient Mediterranean culture. There is also a literary aspect of the backdrop that requires the interpreter's attention.

The Israelite faith was rooted in the ancient stories of the creation of the world, the deliverance of a people, and the establishment of a nation. It was shaped by rituals involving purity codes, worship, ethical standards, prayer, song, and prophecy. When Judah was conquered by the Babylonian Empire in 586 B.C.E., Jerusalem (including the temple) was destroyed and the Judean political, economic, and religious leaders were sent into exile. The Israelite religion had to make some radical changes if it was going to survive. It could no longer be a national religion focused on a centralized, sacrificial temple cult. Thus, the Israelite religion slowly evolved into the Jewish religion of the Book.

Long before the exile, religious and political leaders in Israel had begun writing down the stories of their history and the songs of their faith. However, during the exile this process intensified greatly. The stories were collected into longer narratives. The poetry was collected into a psalter. And the diverse and prophetic voices that began to be heard before the exile and

41

continued to speak through and beyond it began to be gathered into collections as well. Most scholars believe it was during this period that synagogues began to appear. These were assembly halls where Jews met to pray together and to study sacred writings, even though there was no canon as yet.

The centrality of the written word that was blossoming during the exile was well established half a millennium later, by the time of Jesus and his followers, who, of course, were Jews. Therefore, when we turn to the synoptic gospels, we should expect to see Jesus and others portrayed as quoting, paraphrasing, debating, and interpreting scripture. However, by the time the gospels were written, Christians were interpreting scripture in new ways in order to ground their understanding of the Christ event in the story, faith, and prophetic proclamation of their forebears.

Use of Scripture in the Gospels

In the synoptic gospels, Jewish scripture serves as a backdrop to the presentation of the narrator and to the speech of the characters in the story.

Narrator's Use

The gospel writers have their narrators use scripture in three primary ways as they tell the story of the Christ event. First, the narrators can *quote* biblical texts directly. Although all three synoptics do this, Matthew is especially fond of quoting scripture as proof that events in Jesus' life directly fulfill the scriptures. One of the most often cited examples of this is Matthew's version of the "triumphant entry" into Jerusalem (21:1–9). The scripture text quoted by the narrator in this pericope is Zechariah 9:9 (and the quotation is influenced by Isaiah 62:11):

> This took place to fulfill what had been spoken through the prophet, saying,
> "Tell the daughter of Zion,
> Look, your king is coming to you,
>   humble, and mounted on a donkey,
>   and on a colt, the foal of a donkey."
>   (Matthew 21:4–5)

Matthew mistakes the poetic parallelism ("and on a colt, the foal of a donkey" is in apposition to "on a donkey") for a reference to two different animals. He so desires to present Jesus' entry into the city as a fulfillment of this text that he describes Jesus as riding two animals at the same time:

> The disciples went and did as Jesus had directed them; they brought the donkey and the colt, and put their cloaks on them, and he sat on *them.* (21:6–7; see v. 2) [italics added]

The second way the gospel narrators use scripture is subtler. Gospel scenes (or longer stretches of narrative) are often narrated in such a way that they are *patterned* on a biblical story or passage. In other words, preachers of the first century and the gospel writers shaped the stories about Jesus in a midrashic fashion so that they mirror or echo scripture. This was done to varying degrees. For example, although Mark does not cite Zechariah 9 explicitly, his version of Jesus' entry into Jerusalem is clearly patterned on the prophetic oracle (but one must already be familiar with Zechariah to recognize the similarity). Matthew makes the link between the entry and Zechariah 9 stronger not only by quoting the scripture text directly, but also by adding the second animal (Mark has only one donkey) so that the echo is exact.

It is only natural that gospel writers would pattern stories about Jesus after biblical texts. Because scripture was authoritative for shaping the worldview of the early Christians, the early Christians wanted to demonstrate, in great detail, that the Christ event accorded with that worldview. The passion narrative in Mark 15 is a lengthy example of this desire. The story of the crucifixion is told in such a way that it echoes Psalm 22 in numerous places. Thus, Jesus' death is put in the broader context of God's providential care throughout the history of Israel.

A third way that gospel narrators use scripture is to shape scenes in accordance with biblical *themes.* In such instances, no specific scriptural passage is quoted or echoed, but a scriptural theme is present as an unmistakable backdrop to the scene. If this biblical theme is not evoked in the mind of the reader, the full theological context of the pericope is not explored, and a significant element of meaning in the gospel passage is lost.

Characters' Use

The gospel writers present the characters in their narratives as using scripture in three main ways. At times, Jesus and others explicitly *quote* or *refer* to a scripture passage or story. For example, in Luke 6:1–5 Jesus' disciples are challenged by Pharisees for plucking grain on the Sabbath. Jesus responds by saying, "Have you not *read* what David did when he and his companions were hungry?" (v. 3, italics added), and goes on to paraphrase the scene from 1 Samuel 21:1–7 to justify his disciples' actions. Similarly, in Mark 12:28–34, a scribe asks Jesus which commandment (in scripture) is the greatest, and Jesus answers by directly quoting Deuteronomy 6:4–5 and Leviticus 19:18.

Second, characters in the gospels *interpret* specific biblical texts. Luke 10:25–37 is the third gospel's version of the pericope concerning the greatest commandment. Jesus tells a lawyer which commandment is greatest:

> The first is, 'Hear O Israel: the Lord our God, the Lord is one; you shall love the Lord your God with all your heart, and with all your soul, and with all your mind, and with all your strength' [quoting Deuteronomy 6:5]. The second is this, 'You shall love your neighbor as yourself' [quoting Leviticus 19:18].

When the lawyer asks for clarification concerning the identity of the "neighbor" in Leviticus 19, Jesus answers with the parable of the good Samaritan. Therefore, Jesus uses this parable to interpret scripture.

Third, characters often allude to or echo biblical *language* and *themes* in the same way that pericopae or longer stretches of gospel texts can echo Jewish scripture. Jesus' self-referential use of the title "Son of man" is an example of such an echo. Every time he uses it, the title subtly evokes the apocalyptic worldview of Daniel where the Son of man is an eschatological, messianic figure. To miss this reference is to misunderstand the title.

Reading for Scripture in Scripture

When we study the sociohistorical background of our pericope, it is not because we want to learn more about ancient Mediterranean history, but because we assume such knowledge will broaden our recognition of the significance of our text. Similarly, our goal in analyzing a gospel writer's use of scripture in a specific pericope is not to gain a better understanding of the Hebrew Scriptures. The goal is to understand how the new Christian message in this pericope is authorized, legitimized, sharpened, or shaped through the use of biblical texts or themes considered to be authoritative by the author and his audience.

The first step in reaching this goal is to determine *whether our pericope utilizes scripture* in some way. Not all pericopae have a specific, significant biblical backdrop. If our pericope does, then we must also determine *how* **it uses scripture**. Is scripture evoked by a character or by the narrator? Is a biblical text referenced directly or does the pericope allude to it or echo it indirectly? Is a specific Hebrew scripture passage referenced or is the backdrop a broader biblical theme?

How we proceed from here depends on our answer to the last question. If our pericope echoes or refers to a *specific biblical text*, then our next step is the **identification of that specific text**. The notes in our *annotated Bible* will most likely identify that text for us. If not, we can use a *concordance* to find the text. (In fact, it is a good idea to look up key words of a biblical quotation or reference in a concordance even if using a study Bible. There may be more than one Old Testament passage to which the pericope's citation could possibly refer or echo.)

Once we have found the referent(s), we need to **read it in its original context**. This does not mean we have to perform a full-fledged interpretation of the text, but we do need an elementary understanding of what the text meant and how it was used in its original literary and sociohistorical setting. Regardless of where the text is in the Hebrew Scriptures, our *one-volume commentary* will introduce us to the general setting and purpose of the book in which it is embedded, as well as help us grasp the specific meaning and function of the citation.

Now that we possess a basic understanding of the referent text, we should **compare the original text with the citation** in our synoptic pericope. Does the character or narrator quote the text correctly or is the citation or allusion altered? (At this point, we must issue a caveat to be careful about making claims concerning a text that has been altered. The gospel writers do not seem to have read Hebrew. Instead, they used the Greek translation of the Old Testament called the *Septuagint* [pronounced sep-TOO-uh-jint]. It is called this because of a legend that seventy [*septuaginta* in Latin] Jewish scholars working independently all made identical translations of a piece of the Hebrew Bible into Greek. Our English translation of the Hebrew Scriptures, however, is primarily based on Hebrew manuscripts. Thus, any claim we, as English readers, make about alterations is based on a comparison of an English translation of a citation based on the Septuagint with an English translation of the Hebrew manuscripts.) If we decide the text has been altered, we must ask *why* it has been altered. Does it appear that the gospel writer simply made a mistake, or was he attempting to create some effect by changing the text? What effect? How does the adaptation serve a Christian theology and worldview?

Finally, we need to **ask *why* the gospel writer uses the scripture reference** to speak in a first-century Christian context. In other words, how does this particular scripture referent authorize or undergird the embodiment of Christian proclamation in this particular pericope? How does the content and function of the Hebrew scripture text relate to the content and function of the gospel pericope?

If our pericope refers to a *Hebrew scripture theme* instead of a specific biblical text, then the step that follows the recognition that our pericope utilizes scripture is the **identification of that theme**. This is not always easily done. Our *study Bible* may point us toward this theme. However, we will also need to use a *concordance* to explore whether the vocabulary of our pericope echoes scriptural language and themes. The problem is that not all themes are easily linked to specific vocabulary. Our *commentary* may also point us toward a subtle scriptural backdrop for our text. In this step we are looking less for a specific Hebrew scripture passage referenced in our pericope than for numerous Hebrew scripture passages that illustrate a theme referenced in our pericope. (Again, we warn against turning to commentaries too early in the exegetical process, for fear that it will prejudice our own interpretive work.)

Once we have identified a possible Hebrew scripture theme, we should **look up this theme in a Bible dictionary**. Some themes may not have an entry dedicated to them, especially in a *one-volume dictionary*. Nevertheless, essays on related issues or themes will often be helpful.

Finally, we need to **ask *why* the gospel writer echoes the scriptural theme** to speak in a first-century Christian context. In other words—as with specific biblical references—we ask how this particular theme authorizes or undergirds the embodiment of Christian proclamation in this particular pericope. How does this *traditional* theme affect the narration of the good news? How does our recognition of the presence of this theme effect a new hearing of our pericope?

Example Pericope: Matthew 12:46–50
Determination that Scripture Is Being Used

As we turn to our example pericope, we begin by determining whether scripture is utilized in this scene. It is immediately evident that neither the narrator nor any character references scripture directly (i.e., by quoting a Hebrew scripture text). Nor do the notes in our annotated Bible point to a Hebrew scripture passage upon which this pericope is shaped or patterned. Thus, we must explore whether scripture plays a subtler, perhaps thematic, role as a backdrop for the scene. Would the focus of the scene have evoked a scriptural story, passage, or theme in the minds of readers familiar with Jewish scripture?

Our exploration of the sociohistorical background of the passage has actually already pointed us toward the theme of loyalty and responsibility to one's family as a possible biblical backdrop for our pericope. In fact, the *Bible dictionary* essay on the family used scripture references to support its description of the sociological significance and structure of the ancient family. At one point the essay stated,

> Children were expected to honor and obey their parents, and failure to do so was a serious matter (Exod. 20:12; 21:15, 17; Lev. 20:9; Deut. 27:16; Prov. 30:17).

We should look up the example texts to understand how this assertion is made:

> Honor your *father* and your *mother*, so that your days may be long in the land that the LORD your God is giving you. (Exodus 20:12)

> Whoever strikes *father* or *mother* shall be put to death. (Exodus 21:15)

> Whoever curses *father* or *mother* shall be put to death. (Exodus 21:17)

> All who curse *father* or *mother* shall be put to death; having cursed *father* or *mother*, their blood is upon them. (Leviticus 20:9)

> Cursed be anyone who dishonors *father* or *mother*. All the people shall say, "Amen!" (Deuteronomy 27:16)

> The eye that mocks a *father* and scorns to obey a *mother* will be pecked out by the ravens of the valley and eaten by the vultures. (Proverbs 30:17)

These passages demonstrate both the scriptural commandment to honor parents and the scriptural disdain of those who do not. Since our Bible dictionary provided scriptural references as examples, we need to look for this theme in a *concordance* in order to determine how widespread it is throughout Hebrew Scripture. By looking up familial terms and skimming the list of references for texts that speak of honoring parents and being loyal to family, we find that these following texts are similar to the representative passages above:

You shall each revere your *mother* and *father*, and you shall keep my sabbaths: I am the LORD your God. (Leviticus 19:3)

Honor your *father* and your *mother*, as the LORD your God commanded you, so that your days may be long and that it may go well with you in the land that the LORD your God is giving you. (Deuteronomy 5:16)

If someone has a stubborn and rebellious *son* who will not obey his *father* and *mother*, who does not heed them when they discipline him, then his *father* and his *mother* shall take hold of him and bring him out to the elders of his town at the gate of that place. They shall say to the elders of his town, "This *son* of ours is stubborn and rebellious. He will not obey us. He is a glutton and a drunkard." Then all the men of the town shall stone him to death. So you shall purge the evil from your midst; and all Israel will hear, and be afraid. (Deuteronomy 21:18–21)

[In Psalm 50, God condemns the evil of breaking God's torah, which includes:] You sit and speak against your *kin*; you slander your own *mother's child.* (Psalm 50:20)

A wise child makes a glad *father*, but the foolish despise their *mothers.* (Proverbs 15:20)

Those who do violence to their *father* and chase away their *mother* are *children* who cause shame and bring reproach. (Proverbs 19:26)

If you curse *father* or *mother*, your lamp will go out in utter darkness. (Proverbs 20:20)

Listen to your *father* who begot you, and do not despise your *mother* when she is old. (Proverbs 23:22)

Anyone who robs *father* or *mother* and says, "That is no crime," is partner to a thug. (Proverbs 28:24)

[Listed with the hypocritical, the proud, and the greedy as reprehensible is:] There are those who curse their *fathers* and do not bless their *mothers.* (Proverbs 30:11)

[Ezekiel 22 is an oracle of judgment against Jerusalem that lists the city's sins, including:] *Father* and *mother* are treated with contempt in you. (Ezekiel 22:7)

> [Micah describes the corruption of the people, which includes the breaking of family ties:] Put no trust in a friend, have no confidence in a loved one; guard the doors of your mouth from her who lies in your embrace; for the *son* treats the *father* with contempt, the *daughter* rises up against her *mother*, the *daughter-in-law* against *her mother-in-law*; your enemies are members of your own household. (Micah 7:5–6)

These passages, which come from legal, wisdom, and prophetic materials, demonstrate the importance placed on the principle of familial loyalty, especially honoring one's parents, throughout the Hebrew Scriptures. The command to honor parents is repeated three times in Hebrew scripture and lies behind the numerous texts that include indictments, curses, and proscriptions for punishment—even capital punishment—directed against children who do not follow the commandment.

Our concordance quest uncovered some other interesting passages as well.

> A *son* honors his *father*, and servants their master. If then I am a *father*, where is the honor due me? And if I am a master, where is the respect due me? says the LORD of hosts to you, O priests, who despise my name. (Malachi 1:6)

In this text the principle of honoring one's parents is used by a prophet as a theological analogy for how God is to be honored (Malachi 1:6). Thus, Malachi presents obedience to God and obedience to parents as being similar. There are other places in the Hebrew Scriptures, however, that present situations where loyalty to family is in conflict with obedience to God:

> If anyone secretly entices you—even if it is your *brother*, your *father's son* or your *mother's son*, or your own *son* or *daughter*, or the *wife* you embrace, or your most intimate friend—saying, "Let us go worship other gods,"… you must not yield to or heed any such persons. Show them no pity or compassion and do not shield them. But you shall surely kill them; your own hand shall be first against them to execute them, and afterwards the hand of all the people. (Deuteronomy 13:6–9)

> [When Moses discovers that the Israelites have made and worshiped a golden calf, he orders the Levites:] "Thus says

the LORD, the God of Israel, 'Put your sword on your side, each of you! Go back and forth from gate to gate throughout the camp, and each of you kill your *brother*, your friend, and your neighbor.'" The sons of Levi did as Moses commanded, and about three thousand of the people fell on that day. Moses said, "Today you have ordained yourselves for the service of the LORD, each one at the cost of a *son* or a *brother*, and so have brought a blessing on yourselves this day." (Exodus 32:27–29)

[Numbers 6 describes the nazirites' duties to God, which require maintaining purity even in the face of family obligations:] All the days that they separate themselves to the LORD they shall not go near a corpse. Even if their *father* or *mother*, *brother* or *sister*, should die, they may not defile themselves; because their consecration to God is upon the head. All their days as nazirites they are holy to the LORD. (6:6–8; cf. Leviticus 21:1–4; Ezekiel 44–25, where a priest may defile himself to bury family)

[Deuteronomy 33 comprises Moses' blessing on the tribes of Israel just before his death. In his blessing of the Levites, Moses says:] And of Levi he said: Give to Levi your Thummim, and your Urim to your loyal one, whom you tested at Massah, with whom you contended at the waters of Meribah; who said of his *father* and *mother*, "I regard them not"; he ignored his *kin*, and did not acknowledge his *children*. For they observed your word, and kept your covenant. (Deuteronomy 33:8–9; cf. Exodus 32:27–29 above)

In these passages we find that obedience to God requires turning away from family only in the most extraordinary circumstances: when relatives are seducing you into idolatry or have been seduced into it themselves, or when you have taken the radical vows of a nazirite. In other words, obedience/loyalty to family is extremely important, but is secondary to obedience/loyalty to God.

Why Is this Scriptural Theme Used?

Usually our next step would be to look up this theme in a *Bible dictionary*, but this is unnecessary because we used a Bible dictionary in identifying the thematic backdrop of our passage in the first place (although it would be appropriate to look up things like "nazirite" if the interpreter needs greater definition).

Therefore, we are ready to ask *why* the gospel writer echoes the theme of honoring parents or loyalty to family in Matthew 12:46–50. What is the effect of building this scene in front of this particular biblical backdrop? To first-century readers, Jesus' redefinition of family would have sounded quite strong in that it overturned social conventions. But more, it would have been striking, even appalling, to people of faith in that it runs counter to one of the Ten Commandments. If torah instructs that those who strike, curse, or simply refuse to obey their parents be put to death, what does one who completely denies his relationship to his mother and siblings (as Jesus does) deserve? If a scriptural rationale lies behind Jesus' redefinition, then the gospel writer is presenting Jesus as being in extraordinary circumstances analogous to combating idolatry or taking a nazirite vow (although not identical with either). Jesus' act of familial disloyalty takes a back seat to his (and his disciples'?) radical loyalty to God (i.e., his *Father* in heaven).

By identifying and analyzing the biblical theme of honoring parents or loyalty to family as the literary backdrop for Matthew 12:46–50, the nature of Jesus' redefinition of family appears even more radical than it did in our sociohistorical investigation of the pericope. Likewise, the importance the pericope places on the disciples as Jesus' new core community is also increased. Thus, in this exegetical step we have uncovered a deeper level of meaning in our example text. We have yet to explore that meaning fully, but the sociohistorical and literary backgrounds have pointed us to it and prepared us for the next step of that exploration.

For Further Reading

Evans, Craig A., and Shemaryahu Talmon, eds. *The Quest for Context and Meaning: Studies in Biblical Intertextuality in Honor of James A. Sanders.* New York/Leiden: Brill, 1997.

CHAPTER 4

Form and Function

Biblical scholarship was radically transformed in the eighteenth century when the Enlightenment introduced a scientific epistemology that came to dominate all walks of life in the Western world. Knowledge that could be tested and proven was the only knowledge to be trusted. Therefore, in the church, revealed theology was to a great extent replaced with natural theology. And in the academic setting the Bible became the subject of intense historical, critical examination. This process resulted in biblical scholars' growing less and less confident that the Bible contained accurate historical accounts of the events it narrated. In an age when the observable, explainable phenomena were considered most real, stories of supernatural events were dismissed as primitive and mythical. This created a crisis for Christians who strove to embrace both the modern worldview and the biblical faith.

One approach scholars pursued in an attempt to overcome this crisis was to root faith and theology less in the history described in the Bible and more in the history *behind* the Bible. In terms of the story of Jesus, this meant harmonizing the four gospels and removing the layers of myth and legend from the text in order to reconstruct the historical Jesus over against the picture of Jesus Christ found in the narratives. In the nineteenth century, many New Testament scholars produced "Lives of Jesus" that claimed to lay bare the real Jesus, his real preaching, and the real things he did. In 1906, however, Albert Schweitzer published *The Quest of the Historical Jesus*, which meticulously demonstrated that all these biographies of the historical Jesus were little more than projections of a modern worldview onto the ancient Jesus. Instead of true *re*-constructions, these attempts were theologically biased constructions of a Jesus who reflected the concerns of nineteenth-century liberal theologies. At the end of his work, Schweitzer offered some of his own suggestions, picturing the historical Jesus as a thoroughgoing apocalyptic preacher. Although that image was adopted by scholarship to some degree, the primary effect of the monograph was that most scholars abandoned the quest, now believing it impossible to get all the way back to the historical Jesus. Instead, they began to look for a new historical foundation for Christian theology and faith.

Form

In place of using the stories and discourses of the gospels to get back to their historical subject matter (Jesus), scholars began to analyze the gospel texts in such a way as to investigate the historical context in which the texts' oral ancestors were used for faith purposes. In other words, they began to use the stories in the gospels to help them understand the life of the early church. If one cannot get behind the proclamation of Christ to the real historical Jesus, then one should at least get back to the earliest accessible strata of proclamation of Jesus as the Christ.

The gospels, of course, were written around the year 70 C.E. and later, some forty to fifty years after the crucifixion and a couple of decades after Paul's earliest correspondence (see Excursus 1). Therefore, in their final form, the gospels are not very helpful sources for the task of getting back to the earliest *kerygma* (pronounced *kuh-RIG-muh*—Greek for "proclamation"). But the individual pericopae that were collected, edited, organized, and pasted together by the gospel writers may well be remnants of this early preaching. Thus, biblical scholars began plucking these short scenes out of the biblical narratives and analyzing the manner in which they were probably used in the early church kerygma.

The dictum from art and architecture that form and function are inseparable was applied to these pericopae in a methodology called *formgeschichte* (form-guh-SHIK-tuh*)* in German. This word is literally translated "form-history," but the English label given to the methodology is "form criticism." This approach operates on the assumption that by analyzing the conventional forms of stories and discourses in the synoptic gospels, we can gain insight into the way individual examples of those forms functioned in the life of the early church.

To illustrate the strength of this approach, we shall examine a nonbiblical example: fairy tales. All fairy tales follow a basic rhetorical pattern (which is what is meant by "form"). The parts of the standard fairy tale can be easily outlined:

> Fairy tales begin with an *introductory formula* that describes an ambiguous setting; for example, "Once upon a time in a land far, far away…"
>
> The first sentence introduces the *hero(es)* of the story. These protagonists are usually children or nonthreatening (often domesticated) animals.
>
> Early on an *antagonist* appears. This character is usually a hoary witch or a wild, carnivorous beast. Often the antagonist appears in a *frightening setting,* such as a forest.
>
> Accompanying the antagonist is usually a *threat* to the protagonist(s). *Trickery* may play a role in this threat.
>
> By outwitting the antagonist or by being rescued by one stronger than the antagonist (such as a prince), the protagonist(s) narrowly *escapes.* Evil is always vanquished, and good always wins in fairy tales.
>
> The story ends with a *concluding formula* as static as the opening one: "And they lived happily ever after."

All fairy tales share this basic structure. Nevertheless, we must be careful not to view these parts of the fairy-tale form too rigidly. Fairy tales can be so short that they can be narrated in less than a minute or can be expanded into full-length Disney animated films, but either extreme will share the same basic skeleton. So common is this skeleton that Steven Sondheim and James Lapine were able to combine stories like Cinderella, the Baker and his Wife, Jack and the Bean Stalk, Rapunzel, and Little Red Riding Hood into a single Broadway musical, *Into the Woods*. They were also able to use the shared conventional fairy tale form to overturn the expectations of the audience. The last song of the *first* act is "Ever After," and everyone does seem happy. The wolf has been killed. Cinderella and Rapunzel have their princes. The baker and his wife have their child. And Jack has conquered the giant. Everything is so happy that throughout intermission, while we are standing in line for the restroom, we wonder what in the world could happen in the second act. But then the curtain rises to find that during the intermission the prince has been cheating on Cinderella; Rapunzel is pregnant; the Baker, his wife, and their child are cramped in their small cottage; and, worst of all, the giant's wife has climbed down to earth to take revenge for the murder of her husband. The reason Sondheim and Lapine can hook the audience so well with the twist of happily-ever-after hitting the fan this way is not only that we know the individual plots of the individual fairy tales, but that we have unconsciously memorized the skeletal form of all fairy tales.

We have done this by rote, if you will. Simply by hearing so many fairy tales, we have assimilated the fairy-tale form into our narrative bones. This assimilation has been so thorough that we can easily produce an original fairy tale on demand. When a child asks us to tell her a story, and not one of those she's heard before either, we can create a fairy-tale body simply by putting new muscle and sinew on the traditional fairy-tale skeleton. We instinctively know the form and flow without having to pause and consciously reflect on what should come next.

Biblical scholars think that ancient storytellers and preachers operated in much the same fashion. They would take traditions about Jesus' healing a paralytic, a boy possessed by a demon, or a woman with a hemorrhage and unconsciously use a conventional form to shape it into a particular miracle story to be used for kerygmatic purposes. They would take traditions about

Jesus' baptism and transfiguration and, using a basic skeletal structure, shape them into parallel epiphany stories. And they would use parables passed down from Jesus as models for developing their own parables, which they attributed to Jesus.

Function

How does the recognition of the use of conventional forms in oral and written culture help us dig for deeper meaning in a synoptic pericope? Although the use of conventional form does not reduce the meaning of all similar pericopae to a single message, it does narrow the *range* of meaning we expect to discover in a passage. This is so because form is so closely related to function. By analyzing the form of a scene, one can identify, at least to some degree, how and in what context that scene originally functioned and therefore what kind of meaning it was intended to convey. To illustrate this point, consider the following examples:

"Did you hear the one about the traveling salesman and the farmer's daughter?" The conventional introductory formula, as well as the traditional traveling salesman and farmer's daughter story line, makes it clear that this is the beginning of a joke, which means this account would function as a piece of humor. The audience knows from the beginning that what they are hearing is fiction and that its job is to make them laugh.

"Pssst. Did you hear that Farmer Brown's daughter is pregnant? They say it was some out-of-towner that knocked her up." Even though the content of these sentences is still the material of traditional farmer's daughter jokes, the different form radically transforms the function of the material. Although a question still stands at the center of this piece of rhetoric, the tone of a whisper, the veiled "they," and the malicious-sounding euphemism for conception all indicate that this is gossip that functions to spread illicit and potentially slanderous knowledge. Hearers know that the content is supposed to be true but is not supposed to be public knowledge. The form draws them into the small group of those who are in the know over against the many who are not.

"Last night in the small rural town of Sylacauga, Alabama, an incident of domestic violence resulted in the hospitalization of a traveling salesman. Sources claim that local farmer Bryan Brooks shot Matthew McLaughlin when Brooks caught the twenty-three-year-old man with his sixteen-year-old daughter. As of yet, no arrests have been made." Again, the content is similar, but now it is filled out with specific details, including times, location, and names. The ambiguous "they" of gossip has been replaced with an equally ambiguous, but more publicly acceptable, "sources." And the tone is neither humorous nor malicious. It is neutral. This form is that of a newscast, and its function is simply to convey information of interest to the public.

The same event is described in each of these examples. They contain the same basic content, yet no one summary of the content could do all of them justice. The fact that the information concerning the salesman, the farmer, and the farmer's daughter is formulated differently in each example means that each one's significance is different. It is not just content, but also form that gives one the potential to evoke laughter and another a gasp, that leads us to accept one as folly and another as truth. In other words, form empowers content to function in a certain way.

Therefore, rhetorical and narrative forms are not to be viewed as the frames in which paintings are hung. They are the brush strokes that organize all the color on the artist's palette into a work that conveys meaning through beauty. To ignore form while one is studying a pericope is to miss out on a vital element of the meaning of the text. Analysis of the form of a passage and comparison of its form with the conventional form-types narrow our understanding of how a passage functioned when preachers first used it in the early church and how it functions for modern readers.

Analyzing Form and Function

The first step of form criticism on a synoptic pericope is the ***removal of the editorial paste***. Our goal is to get back to the earliest form accessible, so we want to get rid of the material added by the individual gospel writers. We can never be sure about all the ways the gospel writers edited a piece of oral tradition they inherited, but there are some types of additions that can be easily identified. In fact, if we are proceeding in the order suggested in this book, we have already examined these types of additions. They are those transitional phrases and changes of setting at the beginning and ending of pericopae that the gospel writer uses to paste the individual scenes into a continuous, somewhat flowing narrative. By detaching these opening and closing connectors, we get to the older, more oral core of the scene.

Once we have put these pieces of paste off to the side, we are ready to ***outline the structure*** of our passage. There are several things we can do that will help us perform this step properly. First, we may be well served to write out the passage completely and structure it on the page in outline form, putting blank lines between the sections of the pericope and indenting smaller blocks of these larger sections. The divisions of the sections and blocks should be determined on the basis of shifts in logic or narrative focus. Because we are dealing with such short texts, the blocks will be very small, at times only part of a sentence. (Grammatical divisions are usually helpful indicators of shifts in logic.) At this point, we are trying to identify the significant elements that structure the flow of meaning. This exercise will get us visually attuned to the flow of the oral unit.

Next we should ***label the blocks***. These labels should be descriptive of both the content of the blocks and their function within the pericope. They should also indicate how the pieces work together so that the blocks of the passage function as a whole.

Now we are ready to ***identify the conventional form*** from which our pericope takes its basic structure. Is it a conflict story, an exorcism, or a parable? To be able to do this, we must, of course, already be consciously familiar with the various forms found in the gospels as we are unconsciously familiar with the fairy-tale form. (The example will introduce us to one form and Excursus 2 to the other most common forms.) We do not simply want to label the formal elements of the pericope for the sake of having a label, however. The fact that storytellers in the ancient oral culture used conventional structures to narrate stories and discourse material does not mean all stories that share a form are reducible to the same story any more than all fairy tales are reducible to a single story in which the names have been changed to protect the innocent. It is the *combination* of conventional and unique elements that makes these types of stories entertaining and/or engaging. Our purpose in identifying the form of a pericope is so that we can **compare** our scene with the basic, skeletal form-type. By doing so we can see how this particular scene is both stereotypical and odd. We can discover emphases of elements in our passage not found in the basic form. We can raise questions concerning the absence of a conventional element from our text. So here we need to compare our outline with the outline of the basic form-type and note similarities and differences.

On the basis of this comparison we can conjecture how and in what **setting** the scene originally functioned in the kerygma of the early church. (In German, this is referred to as the *Sitz im Leben* [pronounced ZITS im LAY-ben], the "setting-in-life.") Would the story have been used to make the gospel appealing to unbelievers or to confirm the faith of those in the church? Would the discourse have been used to teach about ethics of the kingdom or the split between Christianity and Judaism? As we saw with the farmer's daughter examples, conventional forms themselves can be identified with particular functions and contexts. By comparing the structure of an individual pericope with the conventional form shared by all pericopae of that type, we can sharpen our focus on the function of our individual passage within a particular context.

Example—Matthew 12:46–50

Removal of Editorial Elements

As we turn to examine the form of our example pericope, we start by removing the editorial paste from the earlier piece of oral preaching that was used in isolation. Recall that we established the boundaries of our pericope as Matthew 12:46–50, which reads,

> ⁴⁶While he was still speaking to the crowds, his mother and his brothers were standing outside, wanting to speak to him. ⁴⁷Someone told him, "Look, your mother and your brothers are standing outside, wanting to speak to you." ⁴⁸But to the one who had told him this, Jesus replied, "Who is my mother, and who are my brothers?" ⁴⁹And pointing to his disciples, he said, "Here are my mother and my brothers! ⁵⁰For whoever does the will of my Father in heaven is my brother and sister and mother."

We look to the beginning and end for the editorial paste. The opening phrase, "While he was still speaking to the crowds," is clearly wording added to the oral unit by the gospel writer to connect this inherited scene to the preceding section of his written narrative. The pericope ends abruptly with the words of Jesus. The gospel writer adds connective tissue at the beginning of the next passage: "*That same day* Jesus went out…" (13:1). Therefore, for this interpretive step we will disregard the beginning phrase and analyze the form of verse 46b ("His mother and his brothers were standing outside…") through verse 50.

Outlining and Labeling the Structure of the Pericope

Next, we begin to outline our passage by blocking off its movements. First, we notice that there are two basic pieces of the text.

> ⁴⁶ᵇHis mother and his brothers were standing outside, wanting to speak to him. ⁴⁷Someone told him, "Look, your mother and your brothers are standing outside, wanting to speak to you."

> ⁴⁸But to the one who had told him this, Jesus replied, "Who is my mother, and who are my brothers?" ⁴⁹And pointing to his disciples, he said, "Here are my mother and my brothers! ⁵⁰For whoever does the will of my Father in heaven is my brother and sister and mother."

The first block of material sets up the *scenario*: Jesus' family is outside wanting to speak to Jesus. The second block is Jesus' *response* to the scenario. But we can break these blocks into smaller pieces:

> [46b]His mother and his brothers were standing outside, wanting to speak to him.

> [47]Someone told him, "Look, your mother and your brothers are standing outside, wanting to speak to you."

> [48]But to the one who had told him this, Jesus replied, "Who is my mother, and who are my brothers?"

> [49]And pointing to his disciples, he said, "Here are my mother and my brothers! [50]For whoever does the will of my Father in heaven is my brother and sister and mother."

We find that the first movement has two parts that parallel each other. In verse 46b the narrator introduces the scenario to the readers. In verse 47 an anonymous character makes Jesus aware of it. This repetition of the scenario (indeed, near word-for-word repetition) is a formal signal clueing-in the reader to the high significance of the presence of Jesus' family for understanding what follows. This recognition builds on that which we learned about the importance of the family in ancient culture when we investigated the sociohistorical aspects of the pericope.

The second movement also has two parts, but they are not parallel. The first part is a question posed by Jesus. The question stands in striking contrast to the emphasis placed on Jesus' family in the first movement. We have been told *twice* that Jesus' family is present, only to have him ask, "Who is my family?" This contrast needs resolution, which comes in the second part of the movement: Jesus' answer to his own question.

The structure of the pericope is such that the deeper meaning of the passage is to be found in this answer. Each part pushes toward this climax. If we label the parts of our outline, this becomes even clearer:

Scenario
Narrator Tells Readers of Presence of Jesus' Family
Character Tells Jesus of Presence of Jesus' Family

Response
Jesus Poses Question about Identity of His Family
Jesus Redefines the Identity of His Family

Every part of the pericope focuses on Jesus' family. The first movement simply assumes the common definition of family. In the first part of the second movement, Jesus questions that assumed definition. Then Jesus overturns that definition. This closing statement is most certainly the focus of the pericope.

Conventional Form

We need now to compare and contrast the structure we have discovered in our pericope with the conventional forms used by the early church. To do this requires some advance familiarity with those forms. Beginning interpreters do not have specialized knowledge of these forms (which come from another time and culture) comparable to our knowledge of fairy tales (from our own time and culture). But New Testament scholars have cataloged them and described their skeletal structures for us (see Excursus 2).

The form of our pericope is given different labels by different scholars—apothegms, chreia, and *pronouncement stories.* This last label is the simplest and most descriptive, highlighting the fact that in all examples of this form, the focus is on Jesus' pronouncement. The skeletal structure of the conventional pronouncement story is very simple. There are two movements: the setup and the pronouncement.

The **setup** can take many forms. It can be some action Jesus observes, such as a widow placing her last penny in the temple offering plate (Mark 12:41–44). It can include a healing like that of the paralytic (Luke 5:17–26) or that of the woman with the hemorrhage (Matthew 9:20–22). Or it can be a comment or question asked of Jesus by either a disciple (Mark 10:35–45), a potential disciple (Luke 18:18–30), or an opponent (Matthew 12:1–8). Indeed, so many pronouncement stories involve opponents that scholars are justified in identifying a subcategory of pronouncement stories that are called conflict or controversy stories (e.g., in 11:27—12:40 Mark collects together such conflict stories to set the stage for Jesus' arrest and execution).

The ***pronouncement*** is just that—Jesus' authoritative declaration, which was evoked by the setup. It is, literally, the final word of the scene. The setup is unimportant on its own terms; it is included to serve the pronouncement. The pronouncement is the punch line that draws the story to a close and stays in the mind of the hearer. This pronouncement, however, can take several forms—it can be a brief statement, a question addressed back to the questioner, even a parable (which is a form in its own right). The simple twofold structure of the conventional form of a pronouncement story allows for a great deal of variation in the individual pericope's adaptation of that form.

Our analysis of the form of Matthew 12:46—50 demonstrates that our pericope follows the twofold structure of pronouncement stories closely, but develops each of those parts into subparts (see p. 65).

There are, of course, pronouncement stories that alter the structure of the conventional form much more radically. For example, in Luke 5:17—26 a pronouncement story and a healing story are mixed together. The pronouncement is not the last word in the sense that it precedes the healing. In our pericope, the conventional form is closely followed.

In addition to seeing how the parts of a pericope work together, we analyze form in order to gain a deeper understanding of how the pericope functions as a whole. Scholars argue that in the early church kerygma, pronouncement stories functioned to present Jesus' teachings not so much for evangelistic purposes but to undergird the faith and practice of those already inside the church. They applied Jesus' teachings to specific issues facing the church. For example, controversy stories (a subcategory of pronouncement stories) generally dealt with conflicts between Christianity and its parent, Judaism. The stories presented issues that were current for the early church as if

Setup (Scenario)	Narrator Tells Readers of Presence of Jesus' Family	[46b]His mother and his brothers were standing outside, wanting to speak to him.
	Character Tells Jesus of Presence of Jesus' Family	[47]Someone told him, "Look, your mother and your brothers are standing outside, wanting to speak to you."
Pronouncement (Response)	Jesus Poses Question about the Identity of His Family	[48]But to the one who had told him this, Jesus replied, "Who is my mother, and who are my brothers?"
	Jesus Redefines the Identity of His Family	[49]And pointing to his disciples, he said, "Here are my mother and my brothers! [50]For whoever does the will of my Father in heaven is my brother and sister and mother."

Jesus had addressed them during his ministry. All the stories about conflicts between Jesus and the Jewish authorities over sabbath practices reflect more the struggles of the early church than those of Jesus' own day. We can imagine how first-century preachers addressed these issues by telling stories about how Jesus would address them if he were still around (just as people of faith today might ask themselves, What would Jesus want me to do in this circumstance?) or by applying sayings of Jesus to their current situation (just as people of faith apply words of Jesus to modern issues that were not around when Jesus first taught).

Although Matthew 12:46–50 is not a conflict story, it does clearly address people inside the church, not those outside. We have seen that every part of the pericope deals with the issue of family. We can imagine how early Christians might have been torn between allegiance to family and allegiance to their new community of faith, especially if their families did not convert with them. By describing Jesus as pointing to the disciples and defining his "family" in relation to his Father in heaven over against his mother and brothers and sisters standing outside, the early church preachers who used this story may have been attempting to replace family with the community of faith as the most important social unit for its members. This interpretation stands in line with the observations drawn in earlier exegetical steps.

On the other hand, we can also imagine this pronouncement story being used in a very different way in the early church. What if some early Christians did not choose to leave their families but were ostracized by them because of their joining this new religion and forsaking the beliefs and practices of their forebears? To test this possibility, we should turn again to our Bible dictionary. If we look up "persecution," we find the following statement:

> Jesus spoke of "persecutions" coming upon his followers (Matt. 5:10–12; 10:23). This is best understood as the domestic hostility in family and synagogue caused by conversion to a new faith. Jesus did "not come to bring peace, but a sword" (Matt. 10:34), dividing households and causing financial and social loss to his followers. Because of their distinctive faith, Jesus' followers might lose "house, brothers, sisters, mother, father, children, and lands" (Mark 10:29). The problem is domestic: "a man's foes will be those of his household" (Matt. 10:36). (*HarperCollins Bible Dictionary*, p. 829)

Indeed, some Christians were ostracized by their nonconverted familes. To such Christians, Jesus' pronouncement would have been heard as comfort instead of a command or call: Christ brings those orphaned by the faith into a new family with God as the Father. If we find this conjecture concerning the pericope's function within the early church kerygma to be more convincing, we may want to reconsider the translation issue in verse 49. By understanding the pericope as an expression of comfort, we are more likely to accept the idea that Jesus was not simply "pointing" (NRSV and REB) to his disciples, but was "stretching his hand" (NAB and NJB) toward them in the fashion of a benediction.

Our form critical analysis does not (indeed cannot) resolve the tension between reading this pericope as a challenge and understanding it as a word of consolation. We must withhold making our choice until we have explored other layers of meaning in the passage through the use of other exegetical steps. Thus, we are now ready to move to the next step, which will shift our focus away from the early church oral kerygma and back to the individual gospel writer's conceptualization of the good news. As we move ahead, one of the interpretations will be confirmed or the tension will be heightened.

For Further Reading

Bultmann, Rudolf. *History of the Synoptic Tradition.* Trans. John Marsh. New York: Harper & Row, 1963.

Dibelius, Martin. *From Tradition to Gospel.* Trans. Bertram Lee Woolf. New York: Charles Scribner's Sons, 1965.

Hayes, John H., and Carl R. Holladay. "Form Criticism: The Genre and Life Setting of the Text." In *Biblical Exegesis: A Beginner's Handbook*, rev. ed., 83–91. Atlanta: John Knox Press, 1987.

McKnight, Edgar V. "Form and Redaction Criticism." In *The New Testament and Its Modern Interpreters*, ed. E. J. Epp and G. W. MacRae, 149–74. Atlanta: Scholars Press, 1989.

————. *What Is Form Criticism?* Guides to Biblical Scholarship. Philadelphia: Fortress Press, 1969.

Robbins, Vernon K.. "Form Criticism (NT)." In *Anchor Bible Dictionary*, ed. David Noel Freedman, 2.841–44. New York: Doubleday, 1992.

Sanders, E. P., and Margaret Davies. "Form Criticism." In *Studying the Synoptic Gospels*, 123–97. London/Philadelphia: SCM/Trinity Press International, 1989.

Taylor, Vincent. *The Formation of the Gospel Tradition.* London: Macmillan, 1953.

Excursus 2

Conventional Forms

In chapter 4 we discussed form criticism and were introduced in some detail to one conventional form: the ***pronouncement story***. There are two major movements in a pronouncement story. The first is the *setup*, which can consist of some action Jesus observes; a healing; or a comment made to or question asked of or about Jesus by a disciple, a potential disciple, or an opponent. The second movement is the *pronouncement* itself, Jesus' authoritative declaration, which was evoked by the setup. It can be a brief statement, a question addressed back to the questioner, a parable, or a longer discourse.

Because one of the major steps of form criticism is comparing the rhetorical structure of a pericope with a conventional form-type to see how the pericope adheres to the form and how it varies the form, we need to have the same sort of introductory grasp of other form-types that appear frequently in the synoptic gospels as we have of the pronouncement story.

Sayings

Not all pronouncements in pronouncement stories were originally embedded in a narrative or dialogical context. Clearly, individual sayings of Jesus were circulated and developed by the early church. These sayings could be exhortations to moral, ethical action; proverbs; metaphors, similes, or other types of figurative speech (for descriptions of some figures of speech, see Excursus 3); apocalyptic sayings; analogies; or parables.

Not only were such sayings used as the punch lines in pronouncement stories, they were also collected with other sayings that were similar in either form or theme. For example, Matthew has collected sayings concerned with wealth in one section of the Sermon on the Mount (6:19–34). Such collections are often loosely constructed. The interpreter must recognize the breaks between one saying and the next and be able to determine the connecting phrases added by the editor to make the sayings flow together as a single unit.

Parables

Another such collection of Jesus' sayings is found in Mark 4:1–34 and is paralleled and expanded in Matthew 13:1–52 (and somewhat in Luke 8:4–18). This is a collection of parables. Parables, of course, are found in many other places throughout the synoptic gospels.

The parables found in the synoptic gospels do not share as obvious a conventional form-type as we found with pronouncement stories. They can be extended metaphors (Matt. 13:31–33), example stories (Luke 10:30–37), or allegories (Mark 4:1–9, 13–20). But they do share formal qualities that deserve attention from a form-critical viewpoint. First, it will be helpful to choose a definition that fits the range of parables in the gospels. If we were to look up "parables" in our Bible dictionary, we would find this explanation:

> The three elements in a parable are narrativity, metaphoricity, and brevity; it is a very short story with a double meaning. On the surface level it speaks, say, of sowing or fishing, but on a deeper level it points to something else and it challenges one to discover that something else by close interpretation. (*HarperCollins Bible Dictionary*, p. 804)

Building on these comments, I propose a definition that is adapted from one offered by C. H. Dodd (in his classic work *The Parables of the Kingdom*):

A parable is a narrative metaphor or simile drawn from nature or common life, which arrests the hearer by its vividness or strangeness and leaves the mind in sufficient doubt about its precise interpretation or application to tease it into active thought even to the point of altering one's worldview.

As metaphors and similes, parables compare something that is unfamiliar with something that is familiar. The elements that would have been familiar to first-century hearers/readers deal with animal husbandry (Matt. 18:10–14), travel (Luke 10:29–37), labor (Matt. 20:1–16), feasts (Luke 14:15–24), family (Luke 15:11–32), commerce (Matt. 13:45–46), farming (Mark 4:1–9), patron relationships (Matt. 18:23–35), the justice system (Luke 18:1–8), and such. But usually the familiar is put into new perspective or is twisted or broken. Thus, the mustard seed grows not into a small mustard plant but a great shrub/tree with branches in which birds make nests (Mark 4:30–32). A Samaritan, and not a Jewish priest or Levite, is the example of faith and charity (Luke 10:29–37). Those who work only an hour get paid the same amount (a full day's wage) as those who work all day (Matt. 20:1–16). This unexpected quality of the familiar is what especially illuminates the unfamiliar side of the comparison.

The unfamiliar side is often identified in a formula with which the parable begins: "The kingdom of God/heaven is like…" Thus, parables describe Ultimate Reality. Describe, not define. You can't "define" a way of being in the world, a value system, an orientation toward existence as it ought to be instead of how it is, a hope for God's redemption of times to come. A definition is explicit, exact, and comprehensive. A parabolic description, on the other hand, is implicit, partial, multivalent, even ambivalent. It hints at and narrates meaning instead of diagramming and detailing it. It paints an impressionist picture of reality instead of offering instructions on how to be real.

Miracle Stories

Miracle stories demonstrate Jesus' power, confirm his status as Messiah, and serve as signs of the nearness of the kingdom of

God. Although there are miracle stories in which Jesus walks on water (Matt. 14:22–33), multiplies bread and fish (Mark 6:35–44), and stills a storm (Luke 8:22–25), most of the miracle stories tell of Jesus' healing power. Like the pronouncement stories, a basic form of a conventional healing miracle can be identified. It is as follows:

The first movement of a healing pericope is the ***meeting*** of the person in need of healing and Jesus, the healer. As the ill person is introduced, so is her or his illness. (In fact, usually little beyond the illness is used to describe the person.) The description can be a simple label (such as a leper, Mark 1:40) or more detailed (a woman with a hemorrhage for twelve years, Matt. 9:20). The more severe the illness, the more difficult the healing, and thus the greater the threat to success (Matt. 9:18, 23–24). Other barriers often threaten the success of healing in a similar fashion (e.g., others' attempting to keep the one in need of healing away from Jesus, Luke 18:39).

The second movement of a healing story is the ***act of healing*** itself. This act may involve a physical gesture (Mark 8:23, 25), a vocal command (Luke 7:14), or both (Matt. 9:29). The act of touch is especially significant, since usually Jesus would be making contact with someone considered unclean (Mark 1:41).

The third movement is a ***demonstration of success***. The paralytic walks (e.g., Matt. 9:7), the blind see (Mark 8:22, 25), the lepers are cleansed (Luke 17:14). This is usually little more than a statement that the healing has taken place.

The final movement of a healing miracle is ***recognition/testimony by witnesses***. Again, this element is usually a brief note that the crowd was amazed (Mark 2:12).

The overall form of a healing miracle story can be very brief and simple (Matt. 8:14–15):

Meeting	When Jesus entered Peter's house, he saw his mother-in-law lying in bed with a fever;
Act of Healing	he touched her hand

Demonstration of Success	and the fever left her, and she got up and began to serve him.
Recognition	[*This element is not found in this pericope.*]

Or it can be quite detailed (Mark 7:32–37):

Meeting	They brought to him a deaf man who had an impediment in his speech; and they begged him to lay his hand on him.
Act of Healing	He took him aside in private, away from the crowd, and put his fingers into his ears, and he spat and touched his tongue. Then looking up to heaven, he sighed and said to him, "Ephphatha," that is, "Be opened."
Demonstration of Success	And immediately his ears were opened, his tongue was released, and he spoke plainly.
Recognition	Then Jesus ordered them to tell no one; but the more he ordered them, the more zealously they proclaimed it. They were astounded beyond measure, saying, "He has done everything well; he even makes the deaf to hear and the mute to speak."

Or the miracle story can be a mixed form. For example, Luke 5:17–26 is a miracle story and a pronouncement story combined.

Exorcisms

Exorcisms comprise a subcategory of healing miracles, but they have enough unique characteristics and are so prevalent in the synoptic gospels that they deserve separate mention. The first movement is the **meeting** of the demoniac and Jesus, the exorcist. This movement may include a description of the severity and/or length of the possession (Mark 9:17–18, 21–22). The second movement is an **encounter between the demon** *and Jesus*. Two elements that often appear as part of this movement are (1) a recognition of Jesus' true identity and power by the demon, and (2) Jesus silencing the demon (Mark 1:24–25). The third movement is the *exorcism* itself. This act is usually a verbal command for the demon to leave the possessed (Matt. 8:32). The fourth movement is a *demonstration of success*. Usually there is a disturbance as the demon departs (Luke 4:35b). The final movement is *recognition/testimony by witnesses* (Luke 8:34–37; cf. Mark 5:14–17, where the crowd's response is fear).

CHAPTER 5

Theological Editing

The gospel writers collected short oral and written accounts of scenes from the life and ministry of Christ and pasted them together into a single narrative. When analyzing the form of a gospel pericope, we isolate it from its narrative context, strip it of any editorial additions to its beginning and end, and explore the possibility of the function of the original oral unit within the early church kerygma. In other words, in form criticism we primarily focus on the layer of meaning found in a passage that comes from its precontextualized stage.

We now turn our attention to a layer of meaning that is discovered by focusing on the contextualized form of the pericope. Instead of stripping away the editorial paste, in this exegetical step we value the editorial work as a sign of the individual gospel writer's unique theology.

The Editorial Situation

As far as we know, Mark is the earliest written gospel. This means he is to be credited with the initial collection of the small scenes from the ministry of Jesus into a unified story describing the Christ event. He recorded, edited, and pasted the scenes together in such a way that traditional, inherited material became a radical, new expression of one author's theology.

Matthew and Luke independently used the gospel of Mark as their primary source for composing their own (longer) gospels

75

(for a brief description of the literary relationship of the gospels, see Excursus 1). They followed some of Mark's outline, modified parts (rearranging individual pericopae), and radically departed from it in some sections of their narratives (e.g., in the so-called Travel Narrative found in Luke 9:51–19:27). They copied some of Mark's pericopae word for word, modified most of them, omitted a few, and added many others (especially sayings material—most of which a majority of New Testament scholars argue came from another major source for both Matthew and Luke, "Q"). In this situation we see that Matthew and Luke valued Mark enough to depend on it greatly but changed it because they ultimately found it inadequate—theologically inadequate—to address the socioreligious needs of the particular communities of faith they were addressing. Therefore, they put a heavy editorial hand to Mark's material in order to shape the story of the Christ event in accordance with their own theologies.

The method of gospel interpretation that focuses on the editorial work of the gospel writers is called **redaction** (ree-DAK-shun) **criticism**. Again, the methodology and the label are German in origin. *Redaktionsgeschichte* is literally translated "editing history." The reason this methodology is a historical endeavor (like *form*geschichte) is that this step is still interested in something *behind* the text. Even though we are now concerned with the final form of the text, as opposed to its precontextualized form, our interest is in the editor who put the text together. Why did this person who stands behind the text change this wording? Why did he add/omit that phrasing, pericope, or section? What is the *theological reason* for his editorial work? In other words, in this exegetical step our interest shifts from the proclamation of the early church to the gospel writer's *intention* in shaping the pericope into its final, narratively contextualized form.

Redaction Criticism

There are two main steps in the redaction critical phase of gospel interpretation. The first is the ***identification and analysis of the editorial work*** present in the pericope we are studying.

This is done in different ways depending on the relationship our pericope has with the other two synoptic gospels:

Comparing Focus Pericope with Its Source

If our passage is in Matthew or Luke and has a parallel passage in Mark, we simply consult a *synopsis* to compare it with the Markan version and we can see what changes Matthew or Luke made to the Markan text. These changes include changes in both placement in the broader narrative context and wording within the pericope. (It is also helpful to compare the text with a parallel [if there is one] in the other synoptic gospel. See the following scenario for the profitability of this comparison.)

Comparing Focus Text with an Independent Parallel

If our passage is a "Q" text and appears in both Matthew and Luke but not in Mark, we compare our version with the other one. Since we do not have the original "Q" text, we cannot directly observe editorial changes made by Matthew or Luke as we can in the previous scenario. Nevertheless, by comparing Matthew's version with the parallel in Luke (or vice versa) we can gain insight into the unique features of the final form of our pericope. (Similarly, if our pericope appears in Mark and has a parallel in Matthew and/or Luke, we can compare them but must recognize that Matthew and Luke used Mark as their source. By noticing changes Matthew or Luke made to Mark, we *may* be able to identify some Markan editorial tendencies. These would have to be confirmed by other means [see description of the next relationship].)

Examining Editorial Elements of a Pericope with No Parallel

If the passage we are studying is a Markan pericope or appears only in Matthew or only in Luke—in other words, any pericope that has no earlier or contemporary parallel with which to be compared—then there are two things we can do to observe the editor's hand at work, both of which build on our form critical work. First, we ask a question concerning the editorial paste at the beginning and end of the passage we had temporarily discarded in the last step. What intent is being signaled in the way the editor is attaching the pericope to its narrative context? Second, we use our comparison of the form of our pericope with the conventional form of that type of pericope to point to the editor's work. Why has he modified this part of the form or added that element to it?

The second step of redaction criticism is the comparison of the editorial work we have discovered in our pericope with the **editorial patterns found throughout the gospel**. This exercise will help us see the theological import of editorial work in our passage by connecting it with broader theological motifs in the gospel. To some degree we must rely on the experts on our gospel to inform us about these editorial patterns and theological motifs. The introductions to the gospel and notes on our pericope in our annotated Bible, introductions in our commentary, and discussion of our passage in the commentary should all help us view the editorial changes we have found in their broader context. But, again, we should be careful not to become too dependent on the work of others. After all, our goal is to discover *our* interpretation of the passage, not just to understand someone else's interpretation of it.

So where do we turn to investigate the editorial patterns of a synoptic gospel? First, we turn to our *concordance*. We need to look up every significant word, topic (which means we may need to consider synonyms), character, and place in our passage to see how it is used throughout the gospel. The same advice that was offered when we considered what was significant enough to merit our attention in the sociohistorical step applies here: Look up more than at first seems important. Small things become significant when used repeatedly. For example, in a Markan pericope you probably would not think the word *immediately* is important enough to look up in a concordance, but if you went to the trouble to do so, you would find that it appears in Mark twenty-seven times, and most of the occurrences are concentrated in the first nine chapters. So the use of *immediately* gives not only a rushed feel to the action within an individual Markan pericope, it is part of an editorial pattern in which Mark describes the action of Jesus' ministry as speeding along from event to event.

Second, we need to *read the entire gospel* through to discover editorial patterns that are more linked to themes than to vocabulary. If someone is interested in interpretation at the level we are discussing in this book, he or she is likely to have already read the gospels through and become familiar with some of their major themes and patterns. But it is suggested that as part of this exegetical step we read Matthew, Mark, or Luke through quickly in one sitting, with an eye particularly attentive to the kinds of editorial emphases we have found in our pericope. Note anything that shares wording, ideas, or themes with our passage. (Indeed, this step may lead us to identify editorial elements in our pericope that we had assumed to be traditional elements in the previous step.) Returning to our example concerning Mark's use of *immediately,* by reading through Mark we would realize that the rushing effect supports Mark's apocalyptic sense of urgency set forth in the summary of Jesus' preaching in 1:15:

> "The time is fulfilled, and the kingdom of God has come near; repent, and believe in the good news."

Since the first half of Mark focuses on Jesus' preaching ministry in Galilee, it is natural that the use of *immediately* is concentrated in the early chapters of the narrative.

Analysis of the editorial work within the pericope and identification of editorial patterns throughout the gospel are the two parts of redaction criticism. This redaction critical step of interpretation is fairly easy to describe, but this does not mean it is a quick step to perform. It is a detailed process that, when done thoroughly, offers the interpreter great insight into the theological depth of a pericope. This can best be seen when we apply it to our example text.

Example: Matthew 12:46–50

Identification of Matthew's Editorial Work in the Pericope

We start the redaction criticism by analyzing the editorial work within our pericope. This is done by comparing our pericope with parallel texts in the other synoptic gospels with the help of a synopsis. Using Throckmorton's *Gospel Parallels*, we find that Matthew 12:46–50 is pericope 89 on page 73 and is titled "Jesus' True Relatives." The text is laid out in the following fashion in the box on page 81.

Immediately, we notice that all three gospels contain this pericope, which means we are dealing with the first scenario described earlier. Our Matthean passage had the Markan version as its source, so in our comparison we are primarily interested in observing how Matthew edited Mark's text. However, Luke also used Mark's text as the source of his version, so we will want to glance at Luke's editorial work in order to highlight Matthew's unique qualities all the more.

The first thing we should notice in our comparisons is the *headings*. In pericope 89, the headings for the Matthean and Markan columns are in bold, while the Lukan heading is not bolded and is in italics. The bold print headings indicate that the Matthean and Markan versions of this scene are presented here in the order in which they appear in their narratives. The heading in italics (with the text in italics as well) indicates that the Lukan version of the scene is taken out of its narrative order and presented here for the sake of comparison. In parentheses in the Lukan heading are the pericope and page numbers to help us locate that passage in its proper narrative context as found in the synopsis. (Other synopses will use different fonts and symbols to indicate the same sorts of things.)

MAT 12:46–50	**MAR 3:31–35** ▲ 3:23–30 (§ 86, p. 70)	*LUK 8:19–21*
[46]While he was still speaking to the crowds, his mother and his brothers were standing outside, wanting to speak to him.	[31]Then his mother and his brothers came; and standing outside, they sent to him and called him.	[19]*Then his mother and his brothers came to him,*
	[32]A crowd was sitting around him; and they said to him,	*but they could not reach him because of the crowd.*
[47]Someone told him, "Look, your mother and your brothers are standing outside, wanting to speak to you." [48]But to the one who had told him this, Jesus replied, "Who is my mother, and who are my brothers?"	"Your mother and your brothers and sisters are outside, asking for you." [33]And he replied, "Who are my mother and my brothers?"	[20]*And he was told, "Your mother and your brothers are standing outside, wanting to see you."* [21]*But he said to them,*
[49]And pointing to his disciples, he said, "Here are my mother and my brothers! [50]For whoever does the will of my Father in heaven is my brother and sister and mother."	[34]And looking at those who sat around him, he said, "Here are my mother and my brothers! [35]Whoever does the will of God is my brother and sister and mother."	*"My mother and my brothers are those who hear the word of God and do it."*

We begin with our comparison of Matthew and Mark and concentrate at first on the issue of *placement.* Just because the synopsis here presents both the Matthean and Markan versions in their proper order does not mean that the two versions share the same context. If we look at the preceding pericope (number 88, "The Return of the Unclean Spirit"), we find Matthew 12:43–45 in bold and Luke 11:24–26 in italics, and we find that Mark's column is empty. This means that although Matthew is basically following Mark's ordering of his pericopae at this point, he has inserted sayings material (from "Q") in between some Markan passages. Underneath the Mark 3:31–35 heading, there is a note in small print that reads, "3:23–30 (86, p. 70)." This tells us that we must go back a few pages to pericope 86, "A House Divided," to find the Markan passage (3:23–30) that precedes the Markan version of "Jesus' True Relatives." But when we glance at this passage, we notice that verse 23 begins, "And he called them to him, and spoke to them in parables." Even though Throckmorton has delineated verse 23 as the beginning of a new pericope, the reference to "them" shows that Jesus is addressing someone just mentioned by the narrator. Thus, we must back up yet again to Mark 3:19b–22, pericope 85, "Accusations Against Jesus," if we are going to compare Matthew's placement of our pericope with the context of Mark's version.

And this trouble is worth the effort, for by backing up to these verses, we find something important. Mark 3:19b–21 reads,

> [19b]Then he went home; [20]and the crowd came together again, so that they could not even eat. [21] *When his family heard it, they went out to restrain him, for people were saying, "He has gone out of his mind."* (Italics added.)

Mark introduces the issue of Jesus' family in these verses, goes on to describe Jesus' controversy with the scribes, and then returns to the issue in verses 31–35. Although Matthew does include a version of the controversy story, he does not include any material about Jesus' family beforehand. He has removed the sandwich structure, and it is our interpretive task to ask *why* he has done this.

To understand Matthew's intent in making this editorial alteration, we must first determine why *Mark* edited the pericopae in the way he did. Here is a perfect example of how knowledge of editorial patterns helps us interpret an individual pericope. Mark has a pattern of splitting a pericope in order to insert another between the two pieces (e.g., 5:21–43; 11:12–25). By sandwiching one pericope inside another, the editor pushes us to view the pieces as related, to interpret the two pericopae over against each other. Therefore, the text in Mark 3 that we are considering has the following sandwich structure:

> Then he went home; [20]and the crowd came together again, so that they could not even eat. [21]When his family heard it, they went out to restrain him, for people were saying, "He has gone out of his mind."
>
>> [22]And the scribes who came down from Jerusalem said, "He has Beelzebul, and by the ruler of the demons he casts out demons." [23]And he called them to him, and spoke to them in parables, "How can Satan cast out Satan? [24]If a kingdom is divided against itself, that kingdom cannot stand. [25]And if a house is divided against itself, that house will not be able to stand. [26]And if Satan has risen up against himself and is divided, he cannot stand, but his end has come. [27]But no one can enter a strong man's house and plunder his property without first tying up the strong man; then indeed the house can be plundered. [28]Truly I tell you, people will be forgiven for their sins and whatever blasphemies they utter; [29]but whoever blasphemes against the Holy Spirit can never have forgiveness, but is guilty of an eternal sin"—[30]for they had said, "He has an unclean spirit."
>
> [31]Then his mother and his brothers came; and standing outside, they sent to him and called him. [32]A crowd was sitting around him; and they said to him, "Your mother and your brothers and sisters are outside, asking for you." [33]And he replied, "Who are my mother and my brothers?" [34]And looking at those who sat around him, he said, "Here are my mother and my brothers! [35]Whoever does the will of God is my brother and sister and mother."

By forcing us to read the scene concerning Jesus' family in conjunction with the scribes' accusation of Jesus as one who casts out demons through the power of Satan, the editor urges us to see the actions of Jesus' family and the accusations of the scribes as related. As the scribes are mistaken about the source of Jesus' power, so is his family wrong to try to restrain him because of talk that he is out of his mind. By placing these characters side by side, the editor shows that Jesus' family knew him no better than his opponents.

By deleting the first piece of Mark's description of Jesus' family (Mark 3:19b–21), Matthew cleans up the image of his kin. When Jesus' mother and brothers appear in Mark 3:31 we know they have come to try to stop him. Thus, Jesus' harsh response makes sense. His family has turned on him, and now he turns to a new family. But when Jesus' mother and brothers appear in Matthew 12:46, the readers have no reason to assume that they have come for a negative purpose. They could have as easily come to have a family visit or join his band of disciples as to restrain him. Matthew provides no motive whatsoever for their desire to speak to Jesus, and redaction criticism teaches us not to import a motive from outside Matthew's text. If Matthew does not provide us with a motive, then a motive is not a key to interpreting the pericope. In Mark's text, Jesus' response can be read as a counter-rejection of his family, but not so in Matthew. By omitting Mark 3:19b–21 from his narrative, Matthew has presented the family as more favorable characters and Jesus' response to their presence as all the more striking.

In examining Matthew's placement of our example pericope, we have looked at what precedes our passage. Now we must compare what follows. Pericope 90 is "The Parable of the Sower" and appears in both Matthew 13:1–19 and Mark 4:1–9. In fact, if we scan the headings of the pericopae on the next few pages of our synopsis, we find that Matthew 13 parallels Mark 4 in that both are a collection of Jesus' parables. Therefore, Matthew has not changed the context of our pericope in relation to what follows, only to what precedes.

Having examined Matthew's editorial work in relation to the placement of our pericope, we are now ready to look for his hand in editing the *content* within the pericope. The easiest way to note the differences between two texts in a synopsis is to mark them with colored pencils. In the text that follows we have marked Matthean additions and changes with a single underline and have marked elements deleted from Mark with a double underline. We have not marked differences that are simply of a stylistic nature, but only those that may have a significant impact on meaning.

MAT 12:46–50	MAR 3:31–35	
	▲3:23-30 (86, p. 70)	
⁴⁶While he was still speaking to the crowds, his mother and his brothers were standing outside, wanting to speak to him.	³¹Then his mother and his brothers came; and standing outside, they sent to him and called him. ³²A crowd was sitting around him;	Since Matt. omitted Mark 3:19b–21, he must show the relationship between this scene and the previous one.

Not needed since crowds are mentioned in v. 46. |
| ⁴⁷Someone told him, "Look, your mother and your brothers are standing outside, wanting to speak to you." ⁴⁸But to the one who had told him this, Jesus replied, "Who is my mother, and who are my brothers?" | and they said to him, "Your mother and your brothers and sisters are outside, asking for you." ³³And he replied, "Who are my mother and my brothers?" | Matt. omits Jesus' sisters.

Matt. replaces the crowd speaking with a single anonymous person. |
| ⁴⁹And pointing to his disciples, he said, "Here are my mother and my brothers! ⁵⁰For whoever does the will of my Father in heaven is my brother and sister and mother." | ³⁴And looking at those who sat around him, he said, "Here are my mother and my brothers! ³⁵Whoever does the will of God is my brother and sister and mother." | Matt. changes the vague reference to those sitting around him to "his disciples."

Matt. changes "God" to "my Father in heaven." |

Before we compare our pericope with Luke's version of this scene, we need to note those things we have observed so far so that we know what to look up in our concordance and what to look for when we read through Matthew quickly.

> Since Matthew omitted Mark 3:19b–21, even more weight is placed on Jesus' pronouncement in verses 49–50 than our form analysis first revealed. We are going to want to look for family language throughout Matthew.
>
> Matthew keeps Mark's references to sisters when Jesus redefines family loyalties, but deletes any mention of sisters as being a part of Jesus' family of origin. Perhaps Matthew had different historical knowledge than Mark. Regardless, the omission of "sisters" in verse 47 does not change the meaning of the passage.
>
> Matthew's choice to change "those sitting around him" to "disciples" in verse 49 is related to the way he has connected the pericope with the preceding scene. Verse 46 begins, "While he was still speaking to the crowds." We must back up to verses 23–24 to find out who these "crowds" are:
>
>> All the crowds were amazed and said, "Can this be the Son of David?" But when the Pharisees heard it, they said, "It is only by Beelzebul, the ruler of the demons, that this fellow casts out the demons."
>
> The crowds are unsure about who Jesus is and so cannot be identified as those in Jesus' new family. Since Matthew chooses to narrow the reference to "disciples," we should explore the role of disciples in his gospel.
>
> In verse 50, Matthew changes "God" to "Father." While these words might have a synonymous ring to us, we have already seen how "Father" plays on the family theme in the pericope. Thus, the shift seems to be deliberate. This should be explored further.

Before we turn to the concordance and read Matthew through quickly, we want to do a cursory *comparison of Matthew's and Luke's versions* of our pericope. We need not be thorough because Matthew is in no way directly dependent on Luke, and thus no claims can be made that Matthew changed Luke for this or that reason. We simply want to look at the two versions side by side to see if some distinctive quality of the Matthean text comes into focus that we have yet to notice.

First, we look at issues of placement. Luke's version of this pronouncement story is found in 8:19–21. Instead of narrating it just prior to the collection of parables, as is done in Matthew and Mark, Luke places this scene at the *end* of his version of this collection of parables (Luke 8:4–18) and has no parallel to Mark 3:19b–21. Therefore, Luke's version is even more removed from a conflict setting than Matthew's—there is no introduction to the family as trying to restrain Jesus nor does it follow on the heels of the Beelzebul controversy.

Let us turn from context to content. (Please examine material on p. 88.)

If Luke's version of this scene was our focus, we would proceed in a different manner, but our interest is solely in Matthew's version. So our question now concerns what this comparison brings to light about Matthew's pericope (not Luke's). The fact that Luke omits Jesus' referring to those sitting around him while Matthew focuses on disciples confirms our need to look at the disciples' role in Matthew's gospel. Luke's substitution of "hear the word of God and do it" for language of doing God's "will" may point to a Lukan editorial pattern. What this important linguistic change does for us as interpreters of Matthew is to highlight the fact that Matthew retains Mark's language of God's will. It might be worthwhile to check our concordance for language of God's will throughout Matthew.

Related Editorial Patterns throughout Matthew

Now we are ready to turn our attention away from the comparison of Matthew with the other synoptic gospels to searching for editorial patterns within Matthew that influence our understanding of Matthew 12:46–50. We begin by using a *concordance* to track whether editorial vocabulary found in this pericope has theological import throughout the gospel. We will use our first concordance search as our example and comment on it in detail. Afterward, we will simply summarize our other searches.

MAT 12:46–50	LUK 8:19–21	
	▲ (104, p. 80)	

⁴⁶While he was still speaking to the crowds, his mother and his brothers were standing outside, wanting to speak to him.

¹⁹ *Then his mother and his brothers came to him,*

but they could not reach him because of the crowd.

Luke clarifies why the family is not interacting with Jesus.

⁴⁷Someone told him, "Look, your mother and your brothers are standing outside, wanting to speak to you." ⁴⁸But to the one who had told him this, Jesus replied,

²⁰ *And he was told, "Your mother and your brothers are standing outside, wanting to see you."*

"Who is my mother, and who are my brothers?"

²¹ *But he said to them,*

Luke reshapes Jesus' pronouncement so that it does not refer to anyone with Jesus.

⁴⁹And pointing to his disciples, he said, "Here are my mother and my brothers! ⁵⁰For whoever does the will of my Father in heaven is my brother and sister and mother."

"My mother and my brothers are those who hear the word of God and do it."

Luke keeps Mark's language for God, but changes language of "will" to "word of God."

Family: Since "mother" is the first family term to appear in the pericope, we will look it up first in the concordance. (We must be careful to look for all forms of the word—singular, plural, possessive. Some concordances put these together, and others separate them.) The following verses in Matthew are listed as containing "mother": 1:18; 2:11, 13, 14, 20, 21; 10:35, 37; 12:46, 47, 48, 49, 50; 13:55; 14:8, 11; 15:4, 5; 19:5, 19, 29; 20:20; 27:56. We have already examined the occurrences in chapter 12. Now we need to look up and categorize the rest. At times "mother" refers to Mary (1:18; 2:11, 13, 14, 20, 21; 13:55). There are other times it refers to other specific mothers (14:8, 11; 20:20; 27:56). The other occurrences of "mother" are more general and may be helpful in interpreting our text. We will cite the texts and then comment. (By finding these texts in the synopsis, we discover that all the passages that follow either come from Mark or are "Q" material. But Matthew did not include every pericope at his disposal (e.g., Mark 3:26–29; 8:22–26; 9:38–41; and 12:41–44 are omitted from Matthew's narrative). Therefore, the inclusion of language, whether from his own pen or taken from a source, is an editorial choice made by Matthew. We have marked "**mother**" in bold print and have noticed that other familial terminology often appears in the same context and have marked it as well.

> [10:34]"Do not think that I have come to bring peace to the earth; I have not come to bring peace, but a sword. [35]For I have come to set a man against his **father**, and a **daughter** against her **mother**, and a **daughter-in-law** against her **mother-in-law**; [36]and one's foes will be members of one's own household. [37]Whoever loves **father** or **mother** more than me is not worthy of me; and whoever loves **son** or **daughter** more than me is not worthy of me; [38]and whoever does not take up the cross and follow me is not worthy of me. [39]Those who find their life will lose it, and those who lose their life for my sake will find it." (paralleled in Luke 12:51–53; 14:26–27)

This passage certainly reinforces Jesus' redefinition of family in our pericope. As our passage portrays tension between Jesus and his family, this pericope makes clear that this same tension will be found in the families of all people of faith. To align yourself with Christ (Is this Matthew's definition of being a "disciple"?) implies alienation from those you were close to before.

> [15:1]Then Pharisees and scribes came to Jesus from Jerusalem and said, [2]"Why do your disciples break the tradition of the elders? For they do not wash their hands before they eat." [3]He answered them, "And why do you break the commandment of God for the sake of your tradition? [4]For God said, 'Honor your **father** and your **mother**,' and, 'Whoever speaks evil of **father** or **mother** must surely die.' [5]But you say that whoever tells **father** or **mother**, 'Whatever support you might have had from me is given to God,' then that person need not honor the **father**. [6]So, for the sake of your tradition, you make void the word of God…" (from Mark 7:1–13)

This Matthean passage is in tension with our example pericope. Its focus is not family allegiance, but it challenges the Pharisees' and scribes' attention to ritual by asserting the importance of the commandment to honor one's parents. If failing to honor one's parents is to make void the word of God, then what has Jesus done in our pericope?

> [19:3]Some Pharisees came to him, and to test him they asked, "Is it lawful for a man to divorce his wife for any cause?" [4]He answered, "Have you not read that the one who made them at the beginning 'made them male and female,' [5]and said, 'For this reason a man shall leave his **father** and **mother** and be joined to his wife, and the two shall become one flesh'? [6]So they are no longer two, but one flesh. Therefore what God has joined together, let no one separate." (from Mark 10:2–9)

In this pericope, "father and mother" appear in a scripture quotation. The issue being addressed is divorce and has no impact on our interpretation of Matthew 12:46–50.

> [19:16]Then someone came to him and said, "Teacher, what good deed must I do to have eternal life?" [17]And he said to him, "Why do you ask me about what is good? There is only one who is good. If you wish to enter into life, keep the commandments." [18]He said to him, "Which ones?" And Jesus said, "You shall not murder; You shall not commit adultery; You shall not steal; You shall not bear false witness; [19]Honor your **father** and **mother**; also, You shall love your neighbor as yourself." [20]The young man said to him, "I have kept all these; what do I still lack?" [21]Jesus said to him, "If you wish to be

perfect, go, sell your possessions, and give the money to the poor, and you will have treasure in heaven; then come, follow me." ²²When the young man heard this word, he went away grieving, for he had many possessions. ²³Then Jesus said to his disciples, "Truly I tell you, it will be hard for a rich person to enter the kingdom of heaven. ²⁴Again I tell you, it is easier for a camel to go through the eye of a needle than for someone who is rich to enter the kingdom of God." ²⁵When the disciples heard this, they were greatly astounded and said, "Then who can be saved?" ²⁶But Jesus looked at them and said, "For mortals it is impossible, but for God all things are possible." ²⁷Then Peter said in reply, "Look, we have left everything and followed you. What then will we have?" ²⁸Jesus said to them, "Truly I tell you, at the renewal of all things, when the Son of Man is seated on the throne of his glory, you who have followed me will also sit on twelve thrones, judging the twelve tribes of Israel. ²⁹And everyone who has left houses or **brothers** or **sisters** or **father** or **mother** or **children** or fields, for my name's sake, will receive a hundredfold, and will inherit eternal life. ³⁰But many who are first will be last, and the last will be first." (from Mark 10:17–31; paralleled in Luke 18:18–30)

Again, Matthew's focus here is not family ties. Nevertheless, as with 15:1–6 this passage opens with the assumption that one *should* honor his or her parents. At the close of the passage, however, Jesus promises reward for those who leave family for his name's sake. Which is it? Are we doing the will of God by honoring our parents or by turning away from family to become disciples? In this single interchange, Matthew highlights this tension, but does not answer the question.

Now we shall look up "**brother**" in our concordance. We must be careful to look up all forms of the word (brother, brothers, brother's, etc.). They occur in 1:2, 11; 4:18, 21; 5:22, 23, 24, 47; 10:2, 21; 12:46, 47, 48, 49, 50; 13:55; 14:3; 17:1; 18:35; 19:29; 20:24; 22:24, 25; 28:10. In addition to chapter 12, we have already looked at one passage with "brothers" in it (19:29). As with "mother," this term often refers to actual brothers (1:2, 11; 4:18, 21; 10:2; 13:55; 14:3; 17:1; 20:24). There are two occasions in Matthew when "brother" refers literally to siblings in general:

> [10:19]When they hand you over, do not worry about how you are to speak or what you are to say; for what you are to say will be given to you at that time; [20]for it is not you who speak, but the Spirit of your Father speaking through you. [21]**Brother** will betray **brother** to death, and a **father** his **child**, and **children** will rise against **parents** and have them put to death; [22]and you will be hated by all because of my name.

In this passage Jesus is addressing the persecution of those he sends out to heal and proclaim the good news. Now it is not the Christian who breaks the familial ties, but relatives who will betray their Christian family members.

> [22:23]The same day some Sadducees came to him, saying there is no resurrection; and they asked him a question, saying, [24]"Teacher, Moses said, 'If a man dies childless, his **brother** shall marry the widow, and raise up **children** for his **brother**.' [25]Now there were seven **brothers** among us; the first married, and died childless, leaving the widow to his **brother**. [26]The second did the same, so also the third, down to the seventh. [27]Last of all, the woman herself died. [28]In the resurrection, then, whose **wife** of the seven will she be? For all of them had married her." [29]Jesus answered them, "You are wrong, because you know neither the scriptures nor the power of God. [30]For in the resurrection they neither marry nor are given in marriage, but are like angels in heaven. [31]And as for the resurrection of the dead, have you not read what was said to you by God, [32]'I am the God of Abraham, the God of Isaac, and the God of Jacob'? He is God not of the dead, but of the living."

This passage is concerned with the resurrection of the dead and at first seems to offer no insight into the issues we are exploring. But in verse 30 we see that Jesus' interpretation of the resurrection includes the erasure of traditional familial lines. Thus, the redefining of family in Matthew 12:46–50 is a foreshadowing of the eschatological reorientation of creation.

The remaining references use "brother" in a different manner.

⁵:²¹"You have heard that it was said to those of ancient times, 'You shall not murder'; and 'whoever murders shall be liable to judgment.' ²²But I say to you that if you are angry with a **brother or sister**, you will be liable to judgment; and if you insult a **brother or sister**, you will be liable to the council; and if you say, 'You fool,' you will be liable to the hell of fire. ²³So when you are offering your gift at the altar, if you remember that your **brother or sister** has something against you, ²⁴leave your gift there before the altar and go; first be reconciled to your brother or sister, and then come and offer your gift. ²⁵Come to terms quickly with your accuser while you are on the way to court with him, or your accuser may hand you over to the judge, and the judge to the guard, and you will be thrown into prison. ²⁶Truly I tell you, you will never get out until you have paid the last penny..."

⁵:⁴³"You have heard that it was said, 'You shall love your neighbor and hate your enemy.' ⁴⁴But I say to you, Love your enemies and pray for those who persecute you, ⁴⁵so that you may be **children of your Father** in heaven; for he makes his sun rise on the evil and on the good, and sends rain on the righteous and on the unrighteous. ⁴⁶For if you love those who love you, what reward do you have? Do not even the tax collectors do the same? ⁴⁷And if you greet only your **brothers and sisters**, what more are you doing than others? Do not even the Gentiles do the same?"

¹⁸:²¹Then Peter came and said to him, "Lord, if another member of the church sins against me, how often should I forgive? As many as seven times?" ²²Jesus said to him, "Not seven times, but, I tell you, seventy-seven times. ²³For this reason the kingdom of heaven may be compared to a king who wished to settle accounts with his slaves. ²⁴When he began the reckoning, one who owed him ten thousand talents was brought to him; ²⁵and, as he could not pay, his lord ordered him to be sold, together with his wife and children and all his possessions, and payment to be made. ²⁶So the slave fell on his knees before him, saying, 'Have patience with me, and I will pay you everything.' ²⁷And out of pity for him, the lord of that slave released him and forgave him the debt. ²⁸But that same slave, as he went out, came upon one of his fellow slaves who owed him a hundred denarii; and seizing him by the throat,

he said, 'Pay what you owe.' [29]Then his fellow slave fell down and pleaded with him, 'Have patience with me, and I will pay you.' [30]But he refused; then he went and threw him into prison until he would pay the debt. [31]When his fellow slaves saw what had happened, they were greatly distressed, and they went and reported to their lord all that had taken place. [32]Then his lord summoned him and said to him, 'You wicked slave! I forgave you all that debt because you pleaded with me. [33]Should you not have had mercy on your fellow slave, as I had mercy on you?' [34]And in anger his lord handed him over to be tortured until he would pay his entire debt. [35]So my heavenly Father will also do to every one of you, if you do not forgive your **brother or sister** from your heart."

[28:9]Suddenly Jesus met them and said, "Greetings!" And they came to him, took hold of his feet, and worshiped him. [10]Then Jesus said to them, "Do not be afraid; go and tell **my brothers** to go to Galilee; there they will see me."

In these texts, "brothers and sisters" (the NRSV footnotes "sister" in these texts to indicate that the Greek reads only "brother"; the translators have used "brothers and sisters" to make clear that the text is inclusive) is used metaphorically to refer to the relationship between members of the community of faith. Indeed, in the final text the resurrected Jesus instructs the women at the empty tomb to tell his disciples to meet him in Galilee and he refers to his disciples as his brothers (28:10). Further, in accordance with the use of "Father in heaven" in Matthew 12:50 in connection with the redefinition of family lines, Matthew calls members of the community of faith (brothers and sisters) "children of your Father" in 5:45.

We have looked up "mother" and "brother;" now we need to look for synonyms. For instance, if we look up "family" in our concordance, we find one occurrence in Matthew:

[25:31]"When the Son of Man comes in his glory, and all the angels with him, then he will sit on the throne of his glory. [32]All the nations will be gathered before him, and he will separate people one from another as a shepherd separates the sheep from the goats, [33]and he will put the sheep at his right hand and the goats at the left. [34]Then the king will say to those at his right hand, 'Come, you that are blessed by my Father, inherit the kingdom prepared for you from the foundation of the world; [35]for I was hungry and you gave me food, I was thirsty and you gave me something to drink, I was a stranger and you welcomed me, [36]I was naked and you gave me clothing, I was sick and you took care of me, I was in prison and you visited me.' [37]Then the righteous will answer him, 'Lord, when was it that we saw you hungry and gave you food, or thirsty and gave you something to drink? [38]And when was it that we saw you a stranger and welcomed you, or naked and gave you clothing? [39]And when was it that we saw you sick or in prison and visited you?' [40]And the king will answer them, 'Truly I tell you, just as you did it to one of the least of these who are members of **my family**, you did it to me…'"

The NRSV footnotes here that the Greek literally reads "these my brothers." The translators chose "these who are members of my family" to make the text inclusive. Had we not checked for synonyms, we would not have found this use of "brother." Since we have found no occurrence of familial language in Matthew that refers to the "human family," this text also refers to the community of faith. The nations will be judged, not by how they deal with the lowliest of the low, but by how they deal with the lowliest of the low among the Christian community.

Our survey of family language in Matthew has broadened our understanding of the gospel writer's emphasis on the community of faith in our example pericope. Matthew presents Jesus as repeatedly asserting that affiliation with the Christian faith will result in alienation from one's family. At times the alienation will be the result of the Christian's decision to leave family to follow Christ. At other times, the alienation will take the form of ostracism or even persecution at the hands of one's own family. Redaction criticism does not erase the tension we found in our form critical step between understanding this passage as a call to separate from family as part of connecting with Jesus' family and hearing Jesus' pronouncement as a word of comfort for those who felt their families turn away from them or, worse, turn against them because of their new faith. Instead, the attention we have given to Matthew's editorial patterns concerning familial language has increased the tension. It has emphasized that one cannot be part of two families at one time: The church requires such allegiance and such a new way of life that the old social connections will become both inadequate and threatening. Indeed, so close will the new social connections be that Matthew's community uses "brothers and sisters" for its members.

Still, we must be careful not to overstate Matthew's presentation concerning the breaking of family ties. He is not completely consistent. This break with the old is not complete. Matthew does still value the command to honor one's parents. Thus, the tension is threefold: (1) Matthew 12:46–50 can be read as a call to leave family to join with a new family. (2) It can be read as a word of comfort to those who have regrettably lost family in order to be a part of the new faith. (3) It must be read side by side with Matthew's assumption that people should honor their parents.

Disciples: We should not be surprised to find that "disciples" occurs frequently in the gospel of Matthew. As a group, the disciples represent a major character (on characters, see Excursus 3) in the narrative. From our sociohistorical examination of "disciples" we learned that the term can be used to refer to the inner circle of the twelve apostles or to a broader group of followers of Jesus. Indeed, if we check all the occurrences in Matthew, we find that Matthew explicitly refers to "the twelve disciples" three times. Two of the references (10:1; 20:17) represent editorial expansion of Mark's "the Twelve" (6:7; 10:32). The other is an editorial summary unparalleled in the other synoptics (11:1). Thus, we might be concerned that when Jesus is "pointing to his disciples" in 12:49, Matthew wants us to imagine that he is pointing specifically to the Twelve. But the gospel writer uses "disciple" in a much broader fashion in other places. In fact, in 27:57 Matthew calls Joseph of Arimathea, who was not one of the Twelve, a "disciple of Jesus." So in our example pericope, Matthew is referring to the wider community of disciples.

Father: Matthew's frequent use of "Father" as a metaphor for God demonstrates that it is his favorite such title (5:16, 45, 48; 6:1, 4, 6, 8, 9, 14, 15, 18, 26, 32; 7:11, 21; 10:20, 29, 32, 33; 11:25, 26, 27, 50; 13:43; 15:13; 16:17, 27; 18:10, 14, 19, 35; 20:23; 23:9; 24:36; 25:34; 26:39, 42, 53; 28:19). Every occurrence appears when Jesus is speaking. Therefore, Matthew's decision to change "God" (Mark 3:35) to "my Father in heaven" in our example pericope (Matthew 12:50) is part of a widespread editorial pattern in the gospel of Matthew. Our example passage offers part of the theological rationale for that pattern: New family lines have been drawn with God as the head of the family, with God as Father of Christian brothers and sisters.

Will: When we look up "will" in our concordance we find that every time it is used to speak of God's will in Matthew, God is called "Father."

> [In the Lord's Prayer in the Sermon on the Mount:] Our **Father** in heaven, hallowed be your name. Your kingdom come. Your **will** be done, on earth as it is in heaven. (6:9b–10)

> [In the Sermon on the Mount:] Not everyone who says to me, 'Lord, Lord,' will enter the kingdom of heaven, but only the one who does the **will** of my **Father** in heaven. (7:21)

> [Following woes uttered over unrepentant cities:] At that time Jesus said, "I thank you, **Father**, Lord of heaven and earth, because you have hidden these things from the wise and the intelligent and have revealed them to infants; yes, **Father**, for such was your gracious **will**. (11:25–26)

> [Following the parable of the lost sheep:] So it is not the **will** of your **Father** in heaven that one of these little ones should be lost. (18:14)

> [Following the parable addressed to Jesus' opponents in which one son says he will not obey his **father's** instruction but does, and the other says he will but does not:] "Which one of the two did the **will** of his father?" They said, "The first." Jesus said to them, "Truly I tell you, the tax collectors and the prostitutes are going into the kingdom of God ahead of you…" (21:31)

> [During Jesus' prayer before his arrest:] Again he went away
> for the second time and prayed, "My **Father**, if this cannot
> pass unless I drink it, your **will** be done." (26:42)

There are several interesting things to notice in this survey.
First, 7:21 claims that doing God's will is the requirement for
admission into the kingdom of heaven. Thus, in our example
pericope, being a part of Jesus' family is the metaphorical equivalent of admission to the kingdom in this passage. Second, 7:21
and 21:31, along with 12:50 from our passage, emphasize that
doing God's will requires action, and not just speech. Third, Jesus
models this action when he prays that his Father's will be done,
knowing that it means death for himself (26:42). And we should
be careful before claiming that this was God's will for Jesus alone.
Is this not also what it means to be a disciple?

> "If any want to become my followers, let them deny them-
> selves and take up their cross and follow me. For those who
> want to save their life will lose it, and those who lose their life
> for my sake will find it." (16:24–25)

We have explored the editorial patterns in Matthew that
relate to 12:46–50 by looking for the recurrence of vocabulary
throughout the gospel. Now we are prepared to look for editorial patterns we have missed by skimming through the gospel
and looking for themes and language in pericopae that relate to
our example text. We cannot, of course, recreate the experience
of reading the entire gospel within the scope of this essay, but
we are able to highlight some items we discover in such a reading.

> The reader is first introduced to disciples of Jesus in Mat-
> thew 4:18–22. When Jesus calls to Peter, Andrew, James,
> and John to follow him, they immediately leave their fish-
> ing and follow him. In fact, James and John leave their
> father sitting in the boat to become disciples of Jesus. This
> sort of response to Jesus' call, this sort of breaking of famil-
> ial ties (and no longer contributing to the family livelihood)
> to become part of Jesus' community, epitomizes obedience
> to the will of the Father (see also 9:9).

In 5:1, Jesus separates from the crowds, goes up the mountain to address his disciples, and delivers the Sermon on the Mount (Matthew 5:1–7:29). This ethical discourse, therefore, can also be assumed to play a role in defining how disciples do the will of the Father.

There are passages that refer to people who are hindered from joining Jesus' circle of disciples (i.e., his family) because of the difficult nature of Jesus' words (8:18–22; 19:16–26). Likewise, in Jesus' response to the accusation that he casts out by the power of Beelzebul (which immediately precedes our example pericope), he says, "Whoever is not with me is against me, and whoever does not gather with me scatters" (12:30). Jesus' drawing lines between those with him and those against him seems to be an important motif for Matthew.

In 10:1–42, Jesus selects his inner circle of twelve disciples and gives them authority and instructions to do exactly what we witness Jesus doing throughout the gospel: cast out demons, heal the sick, preach the good news of the kingdom of heaven. This sending forth of the disciples includes a warning about persecution that will accompany their mission, which will include family member being set against family member (10:34–39, a passage we have already examined). Again, we find in this passage that being a disciple and doing God's will may result in the loss of life (cf. 26:31–35 where Peter and the disciples claim they are willing to die for Jesus, but later Peter, to protect himself, denies he even knows Jesus [26:69–75]).

When Jesus returns to Nazareth and teaches in the synagogue, the people take offense at him because they know him as the son of Mary and the carpenter, and they know his brothers and sisters (13:54–58). To identify Jesus with the wrong family is to misunderstand who he is and to place a barrier in the way of relating to him.

In chapter 18, the disciples ask Jesus who is the greatest in the kingdom of heaven (as we have seen, entering the kingdom is a rough theological/metaphorical equivalent to being Jesus' family). In his lengthy response, Jesus comes to speak of the church. Is Matthew setting up an equation in which being a disciple = doing God's will = inclusion in Jesus' family = inclusion in the kingdom = inclusion in

Matthew's church? After Jesus' resurrection, he instructs his eleven remaining disciples to "make disciples of all nations, baptizing them…and teaching them" (28:16–20), which are activities of the church.

The items that caught our attention during our quick reading through Matthew have not greatly changed our understanding of the theological orientation of 12:46–50. But they have helped advance the theological trajectory we have been exploring. Our understanding of what it means to do God's will has deepened (obedience to Jesus over loyalty to family, following ethical standards, being willing to die for Jesus' sake). And our recognition of who Jesus' disciples are has expanded: They are neither just the Twelve nor the larger crowds following Jesus, but also the post-resurrection church.

From a redaction critical perspective, this observation is the link between Matthew's community and the Jesus movement. The gospel writer has edited his material in such a way that the story of the Christ event issues a call and/or offers comfort to the church in his day (approximately 80 C.E.). Thus, the gospel writer did not intend to write a story that was an account of the past, but one that has a theological impact on readers who are struggling to be Christian disciples as part of the church, to do God's will, to enter the kingdom of God, to be a part of Christ's family. Indeed, understanding that Matthew presents discipleship as a willingness to break the strongest of familial ties, to do only the will of the Father in heaven, and to lose life in accordance with that will sounds even more radical in a culture in which Christianity has assimilated culture and vice versa. It is no small thing to claim to be part of Jesus' family.

Redaction criticism is an extremely profitable step in the exegetical process. Although it is a simple methodology in theory, we have seen that it is actually quite detailed in practice. But it is well worth the effort. By analyzing the gospel writer's intent in making editorial changes to his source and in shaping the pericope according to editorial patterns found throughout his gospel, we learn much about the theological depth of a pericope.

The tension between reading our example pericope as a demanding call or as a comforting utterance is extended from the period of the early kerygma to the gospel writer's intention. Indeed, themes and language in Matthew 12:46–50 are found throughout the gospel of Matthew. By performing redaction criticism on our passage, we have taken important steps in understanding Matthew better as a whole. We are now prepared to move to the next interpretive step.

For Further Reading

Conzelmann, H. *The Theology of St. Luke.* Trans. G. Buswell. Philadelphia: Fortress, 1961.

Corrington, Gail Paterson. "Redaction Criticism." In *To Each Its Own Meaning: An Introduction to Biblical Criticisms and Their Application,* ed. Steven L. McKenzie and Stephen R. Haynes, 1st ed., 87–99. Louisville, Ky.: Westminster/John Knox Press, 1993.

Hayes, John H., and Carl R. Holladay. "Redaction Criticism: The Final Viewpoint and Theology." In *Biblical Exegesis: A Beginner's Handbook,* rev. ed., 101–09. Atlanta: John Knox Press, 1987.

Perrin, Norman. *What Is Redaction Criticism?* Guides to Biblical Scholarship. Philadelphia: Fortress, 1969.

McKnight, Edgar V. "Form and Redaction Criticism." In *The New Testament and Its Modern Interpreters,* ed. E. J. Epp and G. W. MacRae, 149–74. Atlanta: Scholars Press, 1989.

Sanders, E. P., and Margaret Davies. "Redaction Criticism." In *Studying the Synoptic Gospels,* 201–23. London/Philadelphia: SCM/Trinity, 1989.

Stein, Robert H. "Redaction Criticism (NT)." In *Anchor Bible Dictionary,* ed. David Noel Freedman, 5.647–50. New York: Doubleday, 1992.

CHAPTER 6

Narrative Reading

After establishing our pericope, we explored the socio–historical and literary *background* of the text. In form criticism, we analyzed the oral, kerygmatic function of the pericope that lay *behind* the writing down of the passage. Likewise, in redaction criticism, we studied the theological intent of the gospel writer that lay *behind* the editorial work on the final form of the gospel. Redaction criticism greatly advanced the interpretation of our example pericope as it moved us to consider the final form of the gospel. But now we are ready to shift our attention from layers of meaning of a pericope found behind the text to layers found completely *within* the scene itself.

As with redaction criticism, in this step we are focusing on the final form of the text. However, as we turn to use **literary criticism** on our pericope, we are no longer concerned with trying to discover the author's intent but with listening to the narrator's story, no longer concerned with the history that shaped the gospel text but with the gospel as a piece of literature. By appreciating the Bible as literature, we celebrate the power of its poetry, epics, metaphors, proverbs, short stories, symbolism, rhetoric, and so forth. It is important to recognize that literary art is not just the vehicle carrying the message—the vehicle is the message. Reducing poetry or story to declarative propositions loses the power that a parable has to create an alternative world or the power a psalm has to evoke intense joy or extreme angst. The power of the message = content + literary art. In this step, we will explore the narrative shape of meaning inherent in gospel passages.

Literary Aspects of the Gospels

As we prepare to examine the literary aspects of an individual passage, it is important to be aware of some of the literary aspects of the broader narrative in which the scene is embedded. The first aspect to consider is that of **genre**. What type of literature is a gospel? We have seen that the gospels are historical but are not history. They focus on Jesus but are more than biographies. We have seen that they proclaim the good news of the Christ event, but they are certainly not sermons. We have seen that the early church shaped some of the scenes out of its own experiences and told them as if they occurred in Jesus' lifetime, but the gospels are not fictional novels. We have seen that the gospels are theological, but they are not theological treatises. Again, we turn to Luke's prologue for insight:

> [1]Since many have undertaken to set down an orderly account of the events that have been fulfilled among us, [2]just as they were handed on to us by those who from the beginning were eyewitnesses and servants of the word, [3]I too decided, after investigating everything carefully from the very first, to write an orderly account for you, most excellent Theophilus, [4]so that you may know the truth concerning the things about which you have been instructed. (Luke 1:1–4)

Luke's claim to be writing an "orderly account" offers us the most basic genre information. The gospels are *narratives*—narrative accounts with historical, biographical, homiletical, fictive, and theological qualities.

Narratives by definition must have a **narrator** to tell the story. How narrators tell their stories is dependent on their *point of view*. The narrator may tell the story from inside the story (as a character or participant) or from the outside (as an observer). The synoptic gospels are narrated from the outside, which dictates that they are *third-person narratives*. In other words, the gospel narrators refer to characters in the story as he, she, or they. What is not dictated by narrating the story from the outside is how much the narrator knows about the story world and the characters. In third-person narratives, the narrator may have a *limited* point of view, which means that the story is told through the limitations of what a single character experiences or thinks, or an *omniscient* point of view, which means that the narrator knows everything about the story world. The gospel narrators have chosen an omniscient point of view. They move around in time and place at will, shift from character to character, and know the thoughts, feelings, and actions of all the characters. Of course, they reveal only the information about the characters and the action that they wish the readers to know.

Characterization in narratives can happen in two main ways. The narrator can *tell* about the characters, describing and evaluating them for the reader. Or the narrator can *show* what the characters are like, allowing the reader to evaluate them based on their words and actions. In the gospels, the narrators rarely tell us about the characters. Jesus is the main character, and yet we are told very little about him. What did he look like? How did his voice sound? What did he feel or think? What was his motivation behind a particular action? In place of answering these sorts of questions, the narrator presents Jesus as teaching, healing, and forgiving. As the main character, Jesus is the focus of most of the action, speaks more than any other character in the narrative, and is therefore a fairly *round* character (one who is complex in a true-to-life fashion). But most of the characters in the gospels are *flat* (characters presented with little detail who represent a type of person more than a unique, knowable individual). Most are not named and never speak. With only a few exceptions, the various people seeking healing are interchangeable except for their illnesses. Most of the disciples are never described as acting individually. All of Jesus' opponents look almost exactly alike. The contrast of the stock characters with Jesus brings him into clear focus as the primary person driving the action of the story.

Luke's making a point of the fact that he has written an "orderly" narrative implies that the action of the gospels has been structured into **plots**. In spite of the fact that the gospels were composed in a cut-and-paste fashion, they do not represent a hodgepodge collection of scenes. A narrative reading assumes that the gospels, even though episodic in nature, are unified narratives with a single plotline extending throughout the entire work. This does not mean that there are no asides or even tangents, but that there is a narrative logic, direction, and purpose that serves as the overall controlling principle for the work. Thus, as with all narratives, the gospels have a *beginning, middle,* and *end.* In other words, there is *rising action* containing *conflict,* which leads to some form of *climax* and is brought to a close with some form of *dénouement* (i.e., *resolution*). Speaking in general about all three synoptic gospels, the rising action involves conflict between Jesus and the powers that be. These powers include both demonic (e.g., Satan and unclean spirits) and human (e.g., Pharisees, scribes, Herodians, Sadducees, Pilate, Herod) opponents of Jesus. Jesus' actions, in concert with his proclamation concerning the kingdom of God, challenge the claims of demonic and human power structures. The conflict comes to its climax, of course, in Jesus' passion (the arrest, mocking, trials, crucifixion, death, and burial). At this point, it looks as if the powers that be have won the day. But then the empty tomb/resurrection follows as the true *resolution* of the conflict by revealing the impotence of the powers that be. Nevertheless, in each of the gospels, this resolution is open-ended in that the endings point toward action that follows the close of the gospel. Mark ends with the unfulfilled promise that Jesus will meet the disciples in Galilee. In Matthew, Jesus does appear to the disciples in Galilee, but gives them instructions for continuing the mission that he has begun, a continuation not described in the narrative. And Luke goes so far as to write a second volume (Acts) that tells the story of the beginnings of the church after the resurrection.

The Literary Aspects of Gospel Scenes

Other literary aspects of the synoptic gospels as complete narratives are beyond the scope of our present discussion (see

Excursus 3). Those discussed thus far provide us with a good appreciation of the literary art found in the broader narratives and set the stage for examining the literary aspects of short, individual scenes.

As we began our discussion of the literary aspects of the gospels as a whole with the question of genre, so also when we begin our literary criticism of a gospel passage should we examine the **basic literary nature** of the passage. Is it a monologue, dialogue, narration of action, or a mix of these? Speech conveys meaning in a very different manner than does action. In this scene, does the narrator offer us the opportunity to listen to Jesus or to watch him? If the passage is a mix of types of material (as most passages will be), how do the different types relate to one another? Does the narrator offer the speech material as an interpretation of the action, or does action serve as an introduction to the speech?

Next we ask **what kind of language** the narrator uses to tell the story or report the speech. Is it a terse description that is straightforward and to be understood literally or, more likely, is figurative language utilized? At this point we want to read through the passage slowly and note the use of *similes, metaphors, symbols, allegory, imagery, personification, hyperbole, understatement, irony, sarcasm, satire, humor, puns, euphemisms, repetition, parallelism, paradox, and invectives.* A word of warning is necessary at this point: Some figurative language is lost in the translation from the ancient Greek language and Mediterranean culture to modern English language and American culture. We must rely on commentators to point these out to us. Still, much figurative language is accessible to the English reader, and attention to this language offers the interpreter great possibilities for discovering aspects of meaning not yet uncovered. Figurative language is not simply decorative rhetoric; it is the power of language to imply, to evoke thoughts, and to provoke emotions. We want to analyze each individual figure of speech so that our analysis will inform our literary reading of the passage as a whole.

In the same fashion, we need to examine each **character** individually. We already have precursory knowledge of patterns of characterization throughout the gospels, but there are still questions to be asked concerning characterization within each individual scene. Which are main characters and which are minor? How is each one characterized (by showing or telling)? Who speaks directly or indirectly, and who is silent? Are they flat or round characters? How do the characters interact? Which ones are to be viewed positively, negatively, or ambiguously? If the characters appear in other scenes in the gospel, does their characterization in this scene confirm, contradict, or supplement the characterization seen elsewhere?

The **setting** of a scene is not just background. By analyzing when and where action takes place, we may discover something important about the action or the characters. A healing in the synagogue where scripture is being studied on the Sabbath will have a different sort of significance than one performed on the lakeshore any other day of the week. Therefore, at this point we want to identify the setting (which may require us to look in the passage[s] preceding the one under investigation) and then ask how this identification helps us understand the plot.

Like the gospels as a whole, each individual passage (if it is not purely speech material) also has a **plot**. As with form criticism, when we focus on plot we are asking questions concerning a passage's structure. But now we are concerned with the logical progression or narrative flow in terms of basic plot structure instead of conventional story types. In form criticism, we might have noticed that two forms were intermingled (such as a miracle story and a pronouncement story), but now we speak of subplots. Can the scene be understood in terms of rising action, climax, and resolution? What is the conflict, and how is it resolved (if it is resolved)? Is the ending a closed or open resolution?

Finally, we must ask how the scene relates to its narrative **context**. In narrative interpretation, we are no longer looking at our passage as an isolated pericope, nor are we simply looking for theological connections with the broader narrative context. Since we assume that the gospel is a unified (albeit episodic) narrative, we must also assume that any particular episode plays an integral part in the overall narrative structure and purpose of the work. By examining our scene within its context, we are seeking information that has two sides. On one side is the question of how the context helps us understand our individual scene. On the reverse side is the question of how our individual scene helps us better understand its narrative context. When we speak of narrative context this way, we must answer three types of questions. First, we must ask how our scene is connected to its immediate context. Does it flow smoothly out of or into the scenes around it, or does it represent a shift in narrative logic and theme? Does it share vocabulary, topics, characters, or setting with the scenes near it? In other words, should we interpret our scene as being in conjunction with the scenes preceding or following it (or both), or should we read it over against those scenes? Second, we examine the scene in a broader context of the larger subsection of the gospel in which it is embedded. It is helpful to have some knowledge of the gospel's structure at this point, but commentators should be of help, especially if we take the time to read the introductory overview to the gospel at the beginning of the commentary. Then we shall be able to recognize if the scene appears as part of Luke's "Travel Narrative," as a movement in Matthew's "Eschatological Discourse," or in Mark's "Galilean Ministry" prior to Peter's confession at Caesarea Philippi. Understanding the broad purpose(s) of the section will help guide our understanding of the purpose of the scene and vice versa. Third, we place the scene in the narrative context of the gospel's plot as a whole. Is the scene narrated as part of the rising action, the climax, or the resolution? Does it serve to intensify or more clearly delineate the conflict? Is it an aside that seems to have little to do with the overall plotline? This step may require another quick reading of the gospel as a whole.

Giving attention to the literary aspects of a gospel passage sensitizes the interpreter to layers of meaning not accessible through the methods we have used previously. By examining the passage as a finished work, apart from its developmental history, we discover the scene's artistry and, therefore, its power and beauty.

Example: Matthew 12:46–50

Basic Literary Nature

Our example scene contains very little action. It is primarily a *dialogue* to which we are invited to listen (or overhear). The small amount of narration, as well as the brief comment by the unnamed person ("Look, your mother and your brothers are standing outside, wanting to speak to you"), serves to set up Jesus' question ("Who is my mother, and who are my brothers?"). This question is a rhetorical device, a trick question. Asked as a response to the information that Jesus' family is present, the question implies that the obvious answer is not the correct one. Jesus continues his response by answering the question himself, which, as we have seen before, is the punch line of the dialogue.

Figurative Language

Jesus' trick question concerning his family indicates that language is being used in a figurative manner in this scene, that it is being twisted from its conventional use into a new, provocative use. The familial terms in the passage are the focus of this twisting.

In verses 46–47 we read,

> While he was still speaking to the crowds, his mother and his brothers were standing outside, wanting to speak to him. Someone told him, "Look, your mother and your brothers are standing outside, wanting to speak to you."

When the narrator introduces Jesus' family, it is clear that it is a literal use of "mother" and "brothers." The same is true when the person informs Jesus of their presence.

In Jesus' response, however, all the familial language is used figuratively:

> [48]But to the one who had told him this, Jesus replied, "Who is my mother, and who are my brothers?" [49]And pointing to his disciples, he said, "Here are my mother and my brothers! [50]For whoever does the will of my Father in heaven is my brother and sister and mother." (12:48–50)

The familial terms in this speech are used in a *metaphorical* fashion. In a metaphor (e.g., the king is a lion) the focus is not on the metaphorical term (lion) but on the metaphorical subject (king). The term serves the subject by illustrating something of the subject's nature that would not have been obvious otherwise. A metaphor takes something that is not known or not fully known (the character of the king) and compares it with something that is better known (the character of a lion). A new characteristic of, or new insight into, the focus of the comparison is given (the king is courageous [or ferocious]). Therefore, when Jesus speaks of mother, brother, and Father, he is not speaking literally of Mary, James, and Joseph. The metaphorical expressions are "My disciples who do the will of God are my mother and brothers," and "God is my Father." Thus, by changing the use of language from literal to figurative, Matthew shifts the entire focus of the dialogue. In the first half of the scene the focus is on Jesus' family. In the second half, the focus is on the way Jesus' disciples are related to him through their obedience to the will of the One to whom he is most intimately related. In other words, familial language has shifted from the primary reference to a metaphorical term referring to something altogether different.

Our redaction critical study showed "Father" to be Matthew's favorite metaphor for God. By this point in the gospel narrative, that metaphor has been used numerous times and is not the focus of the figurative language in the scene. That which is new is the focus: broadening the definition of disciples. When they do the will of God, disciples become more closely related to Jesus than his own blood relatives.

Characterization

If we list and describe the characters in this scene in order of appearance, they are as follows:

> The **crowds** are present throughout the scene but take no action beyond listening to Jesus. The narrator does not even describe their reaction to the dialogue. They serve as part of the setting, making it clear that this is a public dialogue.
>
> **Jesus' mother and brothers** never actually appear in the scene. They are standing offstage the entire time. While

they do not perform any action or say anything, we are told of their desire to speak with Jesus. Their presence offstage is the impetus for the entire scene.

The person who speaks to Jesus is simply referred to as "**someone**." This character is completely anonymous. We are not told whether the person is part of the crowd or a disciple. Since the narrator tells us nothing about the character, we must assume that the person's only significance is to inform Jesus of his family's presence and to give Jesus someone to speak/respond to.

Jesus is, of course, the main character of the scene. All other characters are described in terms of their relation to Jesus (except for the anonymous character who speaks *to* him). The narrator not only reports Jesus' speech directly, but also accords Jesus the longest and final part of the dialogue. Jesus gets the last word and is the one who speaks authoritatively.

Although Jesus is the main character, his **disciples** are, in the end, the main focus of the scene. Jesus physically points them out as he defines them as family. Disciples are the ones who do the will of God. It is striking that they are defined in terms of their action, yet they do not act within the scene.

God is not an actor in the scene, of course, but is a character to whom Jesus refers in no insignificant manner. The metaphor used to refer to God (Father) is one that signifies an intimate relationship between God and Jesus and, by virtue of being a masculine metaphor in an ancient, patriarchal society, signifies authority. Thus, it is no surprise that this God is referred to as one who exerts a will to be obeyed. Indeed, the disciples are related to Jesus, the main character, only through their relationship to God the Father (by obediently doing God's will). As the scene is opened by the presence of Jesus' blood relatives offstage, so also it is closed by Jesus' invoking the presence of his heavenly (i.e., offstage) parent.

The characters in this scene, with the exception of Jesus (and perhaps God), are flat characters. They are stock, stereotypical characters. But that does not mean that characterization is unimportant. The narrator characterizes all of those in the story only through *showing* instead of telling. Nevertheless, Jesus (one character in the story) characterizes the disciples (other characters in the scene) through *telling*. The fact, however, that Jesus does not point to them *while* they are doing God's will indicates that his statement has more to do with defining *discipleship* than describing the particular disciples sitting around him at that very moment. Thus, characterization serves a broader descriptive purpose in this pericope.

Setting

The narrator opens our example scene with the words, "While he was still speaking to the crowds" (12:46). The setting of the scene is, therefore, closely related to that which precedes it. As we have seen earlier, in 12:22–37, Jesus heals a demoniac, is accused of exorcising by Beelzebul, and rebuts the accusation. In the same setting, "some of the scribes and Pharisees" (the same ones who had accused him of collusion with Satan) ask Jesus for a sign, which provokes a rebuke from Jesus (vv. 38–45).

In our redaction critical step we observed that Matthew removed Mark's description of Jesus' family's seeking him out in response to claims that he was beside himself, and thus offered no motive (positive or negative) for their wishing to speak with Jesus. The setting shared with the previous scenes, however, does give the scene a feel of conflict from the outset.

Plot

We have analyzed the structure of this passage in detail during our form critical step, but there is still work to be done in examining the plot. Although our scene is primarily a dialogue, it can be divided into *rising action, climax,* and *resolution.* The rising action (or beginning) comprises verses 46–47. In this section, Jesus' family is brought into clear focus. The fact that their presence is mentioned by the narrator and then restated by "someone" indicates their importance for the scene. The middle of the story is Jesus' question. It follows from what has gone before but requires something (an answer) to follow it. In longer narratives, the conflict is developed over many pages and through several chapters, but in a short scene such as this it arrives quickly and can reach a *crisis* at the moment it arrives. Such is the case here. Whereas in the scenes before, the conflict arose from a statement and request of Jesus' opponents, here the conflict comes from Jesus' own question. His question twists the conventional understanding of family in such a way that it calls for resolution. The resolution does indeed answer Jesus' question, but it does not draw the scene to a comfortable close. Jesus' blood relatives are left standing outside, not being privy to the conversation inside. In fact, the narrator never returns to them in this scene. Did Jesus go speak with them (implying that he simply used their presence as an opportunity to teach about discipleship) or did he not (implying that he truly redefined familial ties in such a radical fashion as to reject his nuclear family)? The internal details of the scene are not all tied up nice and neat, forcing the reader to make some interpretive choices (see chapter 7).

Context

We have already examined the immediate context of our example scene but have yet to look at its broader contexts. Reginald H. Fuller, in *The Harper Bible Commentary*, argues that our passage falls in the section spanning 11:2–16:20, "Israel's Unbelief and the Disciples' Incipient Faith." He writes,

> In Part Three [11:2–16:20], the hostility of Jesus' opponents (the Baptist movement, the Galilean cities, the relatives of Jesus) develops, and gradually Jesus extricates his disciples from Israel and welds them into a "church." (*The Harper Bible Commentary,* ed. James L. Mays [san Francisco: Harper, 1988]. p. 963)

This section of the gospel (11:2–16:20) is part of the presentation of Jesus' Galilean ministry in which he travels about the region to proclaim the good news of the kingdom of heaven, heal people and cast out demons, and gather disciples about him and teach them. It draws the Galilean ministry to a close by presenting the early stages of the conflict that will shape the second half of the book and climax during the passion narrative. By reading our scene in the development of the theme of conflict in part three, we come to a better understanding of the nature of that conflict. It is not always defined in terms of Jesus' opponents' attacking him. At times, Jesus himself provokes the sense of conflict in the events of his ministry.

Broadening our view further to take in the gospel narrative as a whole, it is easy to see that our little scene relates to the Galilean section, and rising action of the gospel, in more than one way. First, it advances the plot by narrowing the community around Jesus—that is, by narrowing the definition of those in the kingdom of heaven. A natural relationship with Jesus does not ensure admittance. According to Matthew, it is not whom you know, but whom you serve that matters. This theology is central to understanding the conflict in Matthew. For example, it is significant to note that in the parables discourse that follows on the heels of our scene, the parable of the sower describes how few respond faithfully to the word of the kingdom (13:1–9, 18–23).

Second, the scene plays an important role in the ongoing and developing characterization of Jesus' disciples. The Galilean section opens with the obedient response of Peter, Andrew, James, and John to Jesus' call to discipleship (4:18–22). Jesus instructs them on ethical matters in the Sermon on the Mount (Matt. 5–7). He defends them in controversies, thus drawing them closer into his circle and setting up his opponents as their opponents (e.g., 9:14–17; 12:1–8; cf. 9:10–13; 16:5–12). He gives them authority and sends them out to do what he has done—preach and heal (9:35–10:42). Surely, the disciples are those who do the will of God. But in the climax, when the crisis hits, the disciples, who have supposedly replaced Jesus' family, will desert and deny their master (26:31–35, 56, 69–75). Nevertheless, during the resolution, Jesus will recommission them after the resurrection, this time with the command to "make disciples" of all nations (28:16–20).

When we draw together our different literary observations concerning 12:46–50, we can conclude that the focus of the scene rests on the characterization of the disciples. Jesus' family appears in the rising action only to be used as a metaphorical reference for the disciples in the resolution. The conflicts between Jesus and his opponents throughout 11:2–16:20 lead us to read this scene as a conflict as well. In this scene, however, the conflict is not between Pharisees and Jesus but between Jesus and his family. Initiating the conflict himself, Jesus appears to be defining those related to him in a narrow fashion: Only those doing the will of his metaphorical Father can be considered part of his metaphorical family.

Our examination of the literary aspects of Matthew 12:46–50 has both confirmed our earlier observations and advanced our understanding beyond them. We see that each method we use overlaps with others, builds on the observations of others, and offers something new. There is one more exegetical step that we will examine in this introduction to the interpretive process.

For Further Reading

Malbon, Elizabeth Struthers. "Narrative Criticism: How Does the Story Mean?" In *Mark & Method: New Approaches in Biblical Studies*, ed. Janice Capel Anderson and Stephen D. Moore, 23–49. Minneapolis: Fortress Press, 1992.

Moore, Stephen D. "Gospel Criticism as Narrative Criticism." In *Literary Criticism and the Gospels: The Theoretical Challenge*, 1–68. New Haven/London: Yale University Press, 1989.

Peterson, Norman R. *Literary Criticism for New Testament Critics*. Guides to Biblical Scholarship. Philadelphia: Fortress Press, 1978.

Powell, Mark Allan. *What Is Narrative Criticism?* Guides to Biblical Scholarship. Minneapolis: Fortress Press, 1990.

————. "Toward a Narrative-Critical Understanding of Matthew" "…of Mark" "…of Luke." In *Gospel Interpretation: Narrative-Critical & Social-Scientific Approaches*, ed. Jack Dean Kingsbury, 9–15, 65–70, 125–31. Harrisburg, Pa.: Trinity Press International, 1997.

EXCURSUS 3

Select Literary Terms for Narrative Exegesis

ACTION: *See* Plot.

ALLEGORY: A narrative in which elements of the story (e.g., characters, action, setting) have a symbolic significance as well as a literal significance within the story. Some of Jesus' parables are allegorical. For example, the parable of the sower is accompanied by an allegorical interpretation (Mark 4:1–8, 13–20). (*See* Symbol.)

APOSTROPHE: Direct address to an absent person or to an abstract or inanimate object. In Luke 13:34, Jesus stands outside the city of Jerusalem and addresses it in the form of a lament: "Jerusalem, Jerusalem, the city that kills the prophets and stones those who are sent to it! How often have I desired to gather your children together as a hen gathers her brood under her wings, and you were not willing!"

CHARACTER: Characters are the persons presented in the narrative; they can be individuals (Jesus, Satan) or a group that acts as a single character (the Pharisees).

There are two basic types of characters in literature. *Flat characters* are two-dimensional, built around a single idea or quality, presented without much individualizing detail. Almost all narratives have some characters that are simply types, functionaries (e.g., characters in need of healing are usually characterized by little more than their illness: Matt. 9:2; Luke 6:6). *Round characters* are three-dimensional, are complex in temperament and motivation, are represented with subtle particularity, are as difficult to describe with any adequacy as a person in real life, may develop and grow (e.g., from innocence to maturity), and, like most persons, are capable of surprising us. Jesus is the most developed character in the gospel. (*See also* Characterization.)

CHARACTERIZATION: The way the narrator helps the reader get to know characters. (*See* Character.) There are two primary ways the narrator does this. *Telling* is when the narrator authoritatively describes and/or evaluates characters' motives and dispositional qualities (e.g., when Jesus denounces the scribes and Pharisees: Matt. 23:1–36). *Showing* is when the narrator merely presents the characters as talking and acting and leaves the reader to infer what motives and dispositions lie behind what they say and do. So their *actions* and *dialogue* reveal who they are and what they are like (e.g., we are rarely told of Jesus' motives and thoughts when he is performing healings).

DENOUEMENT: *See* Plot.

DICTION: *See* Style.

EUPHEMISM: Metaphorical language substituted for blunt language labeling or describing something disagreeable or offensive. An example of a euphemism in the gospels is Jesus' reference to his own death as baptism (Mark 10:38).

FIGURATIVE LANGUAGE: Figures of speech used in an imaginative rather than a literal sense; a use of words that stretches or bends the standard use of those words in order to convey a new meaning or effect. Examples of figurative language include *metaphors* and *similes*.

HYPERBOLE: Bold overstatement or extravagant exaggeration. An example of such exaggeration is found in Mark 1:5, where the narrator claims that "people from the *whole* Judean countryside and *all* the people of Jerusalem" went out to John the Baptist and were baptized by him.

IDIOM: A word or phrase characteristic of or peculiar to a particular language. The meaning of an idiom is usually not readily apparent to non-native speakers of that language. English readers of the gospels are dependent on commentaries to identify and interpret Greek idioms.

IRONY: A tone that involves a distinction between the explicit meaning of statements and events recognized by characters in the narrative and the implicit meaning recognized by the reader. The reader is aware of things of which the characters are ignorant. For example, Mark's passion narrative is full of irony. Two examples: (1) Peter denies Jesus for the third time with the words, "I do not know this man you are talking about" (14:71). Peter assumes he is lying, but the reader recognizes that his words speak truth—he really does not know who Jesus is or he would not have abandoned and denied him. (2) The soldiers clothe Jesus in a purple robe, place a crown of thorns on his head, salute him as "king of the Jews," and kneel down in homage to him before leading him off to be crucified (15:17–20). The soldiers are mocking Jesus, but having heard Jesus' proclamation of the kingdom of God and his passion predictions, the reader recognizes the kingship of Jesus and the cross as his throne.

METAPHOR: A comparison of two distinctively different things made without explicitly asserting the comparison. The use of a metaphor expands or alters the understanding of the primary referent. In Luke 13:32, Jesus uses a metaphor when he refers to Herod as a "fox." (*See also* Figurative Language.)

PARALLELISM: In Hebrew poetry, it is common to repeat an idea with similar, yet varied, language, in parallel lines. Such parallelism can appear in scripture quotations included in the gospels (e.g., Matt. 21:5 quotes Zech. 9:9).

PERSONIFICATION: A metaphorical attribution of human qualities to animals, inanimate objects, or abstract concepts. In Luke 13:34,

Jesus addresses the city of Jerusalem as if it were an agent who could hear and act: "Jerusalem, Jerusalem, the city that kills the prophets and stones those who are sent to it! How often have I desired to gather your children together as a hen gathers her brood under her wings, and you were not willing!" (*See also* Figurative Language.)

PLOT: The narrative's structure of actions (both verbal and physical) as these are rendered and ordered toward achieving particular emotional and artistic effects. These actions are, of course, performed by characters and exhibit their moral qualities and dispositions. Thus, plot and character are interdependent critical concepts. (*See* Character.)

Plot is different from *story*. The story is simply a summary of the temporal order of events described in the narrative: First this happens, then that, then that. It is only when we say *how* this is related to that, and in what way all these matters are rendered and organized so as to achieve their particular effects, that we are discussing plot.

A plot has *unity of action* if it is perceived by the reader as a complete and ordered structure of actions, directed toward the intended effect, in which none of the component parts are unnecessary. Criticism of the gospels that attempted to get "behind the text" broke the narrative into pieces. Narrative criticism assumes that even though the gospels seem episodic, they do present a unity of action.

The order of a unified plot is a continuous sequence of *beginning, middle*, and *end*. As a plot progresses, it arouses expectations in the reader about the future course of events and how characters will respond to events. The beginning initiates the main action in a way that makes us look forward to something more; the middle presumes what has gone before and requires something to follow; and the end follows from what has gone before but requires nothing more—the reader is satisfied that the plot is complete.

The action of these parts follows three basic moves. First, there is the *rising action* or *complication*. This rising action is often characterized by *conflict*. Second, the rising action reaches a *climax*. Third, the climax gives way to the *falling action* in which the complication is resolved for better or worse. This closing is often called the *dénouement* (French for "unknotting"): The action or intrigue ends in success or failure for the protagonist, the mystery is solved, or the misunderstanding is cleared away.

POINT OF VIEW: The *way* the story gets told—the perspective from which the narrator presents the characters, actions, settings, and events that constitute the narrative.

There are two basic broad categories of narratives when viewed from the angle of point of view. Stories can be *first-person narratives* or *third-person narratives*. In other words, the narrator can either be a character participating in the story (using the pronoun *I*) or an observer outside the story (using the pronouns *he, she, it, they*). The gospels are all told as third-person narratives. (An example of first-person narrative materials are the "we narratives" of Acts [written by Luke] beginning in Acts 16:11.)

Within third-person narratives, there are two subcategories of point of view. In *limited point of view* the narrator tells the story in third person, but within the confines of what is experienced, thought, and felt by a single character or a few characters within the story. In *omniscient point of view* the narrator knows everything that needs to be known about the characters and events and is free to move at will in time and place, to shift from character to character, and to report or conceal their speech, actions, thoughts, feelings, and motives. The narrators of the gospels are all omniscient.

RHETORICAL QUESTION: A question asked that is not meant to evoke a reply. The speaker assumes the answer to be obvious and shared by both speaker and hearers.

SETTING: The general locale, time, and social circumstances in which the action of a narrative or section of a narrative occurs.

Simile: A comparison of two distinctively different things made explicit by *like* or *as*. Although most scholars speak of parables as narrative *metaphors*, they often begin with the phrase, "The kingdom of God is like…" Thus, they have at times been referred to as *similitudes*. In Luke 7:32, Jesus uses a simile to describe the generation that has misunderstood him; they are "like children sitting in the marketplace and calling to one another, 'We played the flute for you, and you did not dance; we wailed, and you did not weep.'" (*See* Figurative Language.)

Story: *See* Plot.

Style: The manner of linguistic expression, *how* a work says whatever it is that it says. The style of a particular work may be analyzed in terms of *diction* (choice of words); sentence structure and syntax; density and types of figurative language; patterns of rhythm, component sounds, and other formal features; and use of rhetorical devices.

In terms of quality of style of the synoptics, Mark is usually considered to be of the lowest style and Luke the highest. Consider sentence structure: Mark is *paratactic* in style—short sentences (or parts of sentences) weakly connected (by using "and"). Similarly, the scenes are episodic. Luke is more *hypotactic* in style—connection between sentences (and parts of sentences) are expressed in temporal and logical terms and by the use of subordinate phrases and clauses (e.g., Luke 1:1–4).

Symbol: An element in a narrative (person, place, or thing) that represents something beyond itself.

Tone: A speaker's implied attitude toward his or her audience. This can refer to a character's attitude toward other characters she or he is addressing or to the narrator's attitude toward the narratee (or reader).

CHAPTER 7

The Experience of the Implied Reader

The reason people of faith are concerned with understanding scripture at deeper levels of meaning is so that scripture can impact their lives at deeper levels—so that scripture can influence, shape, even transform their views of God, self, and the world. In other words, we interpret scripture so that it, in turn, might interpret us—revealing who we are and calling us to who we ought to be.

Therefore, it is appropriate at this point that we turn our attention to the experience of the reader. We began by exploring the *background* of the gospels and then moved to examine the kerygma and author's intention *behind* the text. In our last step we analyzed the literary aspects that lie *within* the text. Now we shift our focus to the reader who stands *before* the gospels.

The Power of the Reader

It has been argued that when a tree falls in the woods, it makes no noise unless someone is there to hear it. By the same logic, a text says nothing until someone reads it. We have spent much time discussing how a better understanding of the influence exerted on a passage by the early church, the editor, and the narrator should shape our interpretation. Now we need to appreciate the influence the reader has on the text. Regardless of how well an author writes a book or how well a narrator tells the story, a text is little more than inkblots on a processed wood by-product until someone picks it up and reads it. The written word only becomes communication when people put themselves in the place of receiving the communication.

However, the power of the reader extends far beyond the choice to read a text or not. The text is transformed from meaningless inkblots into language as our eyes scan the line and make letters, words, and sentences out of the markings. In this sense, it is not wrong to say that the reader *constructs* meaning out of the text instead of discovering meaning *in* the text. One example used to illustrate this point is as follows: Let us imagine that a professor draws three intersecting lines on a chalkboard that look like this:

When she asks the class, "What do these lines mean?" most students will answer that they compose an arrow that points toward something or gives direction. Suppose the teacher presses harder: "*Why* do the lines mean?" In other words, why do students interpret these three lines as an arrow? Is it because conventional use of three intersecting lines in this fashion defines them as an arrow (as a form critic might argue)? Is it because the teacher intended them to be an arrow (as a redaction critic might argue)? Is it something within the drawing itself that results in its interpretation as an arrow (as a narrative critic might argue)? Or is it because the students have chosen to interpret the lines as an arrow (partially because of the influence of convention, assumptions about the teacher's intention in writing on the board, and beliefs about inherent meaning in signs)? Imagine three branches have, by pure coincidence, fallen in the woods in the same arrangement. Do these three branches make up an arrow? If a hiker comes upon the three branches and changes his direction, it is clear that he has interpreted them as an arrow.

If he continues in his original direction, then he has interpreted them as nothing more than three branches fallen in the woods.

We have not spent so much time in previous chapters dealing with conventional form, editorial intention, and literary artistry only to deny their role in constructing meaning at this point in the interpretive process. But we do need to assert strongly that readers also make meaning of texts. They are partners (not silent partners, but active partners) with those things that lie in the background, behind, and within the text. Based on their understanding (or lack of understanding), readers construct meaning from their position *before* the text.

This fact raises a caveat in our interpretive process. It warns against the assumption that there is a single, correct interpretation of a gospel passage or of a gospel as a whole. The fact that there is a myriad of readers (each shaped by her or his culture, family of origin, education, psychological development, religious training, etc.) implies that there will be a myriad of interpretations. This does not mean, however, that *any* interpretation is a *valid* interpretation. Our whole description of the interpretive process has been based on the assumption that the more informed interpreters are, the more responsible an interpretation they will construct. A student could argue that the three intersecting lines drawn on the board by the teacher represented a still life of a bowl of fruit and a bottle of wine, but it would not be a valid interpretation of the lines. The convention of the arrow, knowledge of the teacher who drew the lines, and appearance of the chalk lines limit the range of responsible interpretations available. By the same argument, while the inkblots on a page do not have meaning until readers create meaning out of them, the inkblots are the materials out of which we construct meaning and thus limit the range of valid meanings we can create. Even though there are many valid interpretations of the crucifixion, it would be irresponsible to interpret the passion narrative of Christ as if it were an instruction manual on animal husbandry or a set of formulas for calculus equations.

Throughout this book we have presented the interpretive process as a search to discover the layers of meaning in a gospel passage. Our attention to the power of the reader means we must fine-tune that definition of the exegetical goal, but it does not mean that it must be completely abandoned. Even while acknowledging the power of the reader, we continue to affirm that our goal is exegesis, not eisegesis. As responsible readers, we still want to avoid projecting our own prejudices and values onto a pericope. Nevertheless, we must acknowledge, at this point, that the interpretive process is not a purely objective one. Indeed, it is an intensely subjective one. This subjective element of interpretation means not only that readers have great power in interpreting a biblical text (as with any text), but also that the biblical text (as with any text) possesses great potential to influence, persuade, transform, and, yes, interpret readers who commit themselves to the reading and interpretation process.

Interpreting the Reading Process

Interpretation that focuses on the reader's power to construct meaning is called **reader-response criticism**. Various reader-response approaches share the goal of analyzing the process of reading. They wish to take the pulse of the reader after each word, phrase, sentence, paragraph, movement, and chapter is digested. What expectations are formed? Are those expectations then fulfilled, changed, or completely overturned? To reader-response critics, the significance of the text is not a propositional summary of the text's content, but the manner in which the reader is affected by the process of reading the text. In actuality, however, there is no agreement among reader-response critics as to how to determine or describe this effect. There is no single reader-response method; there are numerous reader-response approaches. In this essay we will focus on one example of reader-response sensitivities that is accessible to the beginning interpreter.

Before launching into reader-response criticism, we must first define some basic terminology. It is necessary to distinguish between the real reader, the implied reader, and the addressee. We will define these terms in relation to the gospel of Luke, since we have turned to its prologue to help us before. The **real reader** is the actual individual standing before the text. In the case of Luke, the real reader is, of course, me, a modern reader/interpreter. The **implied reader** is the *type* of person(s) for whom the real reader thinks the text was written (the intended audience, if you will). The image we have of this reader is implied from the literary work itself, constructed from clues within the text and our knowledge of the context in which the text was published. Turning to Luke, we noted that the gospel was written sometime after 70 C.E. In the prologue, Luke claims to be writing so that the reader "may know the truth concerning *the things about which you have been instructed*" (1:4). And, finally, throughout the gospel (and Acts) there is a strong emphasis on the gospel's being extended to Gentiles. Thus, Luke's implied reader is a first-century Gentile Christian. The **addressee** of a text, on the other hand, is the person whom the narrator in the text directly addresses. Often, the addressee and implied reader are identical, but not always. For example, *The Color Purple* is written in the form of letters, many of which are addressed to God, but clearly the implied reader of these fictional letters is human. In Luke's prologue a specific addressee is named: Theophilus (1:3). Scholars have long argued whether Theophilus was a real person (who perhaps served as the gospel writer's patron and publisher) or is a symbolic name (*Theo*—God, *philus*—lover). Regardless, Luke certainly writes for a wider audience than a single person. Yet Theophilus is a distinctively Greek name with religious overtones. So although there is distance between this addressee and the implied Gentile Christian reader, it is a short distance.

The type of reader-response criticism we are using in this chapter asks the real reader to **identify** with the implied reader. To do this we must know something of the implied reader of the gospels. Therefore, we must be able to draw a general picture of the implied readers of the synoptic gospels. Part of our picture comes from our knowledge of the historical and sociological context in which the implied readers would have existed. For example,

Implied readers of the gospels in the first century would have been part of the literate minority. Specifically, they could read Greek (although that does not help us as English readers). The ability to read in a society that is primarily illiterate usually implies a certain level of wealth. In ancient Mediterranean culture, most of those able to read would have been men, since the patriarchal structures promoted education for males in a way it did not for females. However, the implied "readers" must be expanded somewhat beyond those who could read. Much of ancient literature was read aloud in community for entertainment and instruction. Thus, part of the picture of the implied "reader" is the audience of an oral reading.

The implied readers/hearers would have shared the same worldview as the rest of the Mediterranean world. They would have thought of the world in a nonrationalistic, prescientific manner, and thus focused more on divine and demonic powers at play in the world than on the "forces of nature."

Being part of ancient Mediterranean society, they would have immediately understood references to things like tax collectors, agricultural practices, geographical regions, and political circumstances. They would not have had the same need for a Bible dictionary that we have.

The other half of our picture comes from implicit signals within the gospels themselves. For example,

We know the implied readers already knew something of the story of the Christ event. This is evident not only in Luke's prologue, but also in more subtle references, such as the description of Judas early in the narratives as the one "who betrayed Jesus" (Mark 3:19; cf. Matthew 10:4; Luke 6:16). Clearly, the implied readers are supposed to understand this reference before they have read the passion narrative. Therefore, the implied readers are not introduced to the Christ event by the gospels, but have their understanding of the Christ event broadened and/or altered.

Likewise, the implied readers have some knowledge of and appreciation for Jewish scripture. Otherwise the gospel writers could not have used it so thoroughly, and at times, so subtly.

By identifying with a gospel's implied readers, we open our-selves to **the experience of the implied readers**. What ex-pectations would these implied readers (such as we have described) have at this point in the narrative? What gaps in the narrative would the implied readers have to fill in, and how would they probably have done it? How would the implied read-ers experience this rising action, this conflict, this climax, this resolution? Would the implied readers' assumptions, values, and experiences be attacked, queried, supported, or solicited by the narrator at this point in the story? In other words, as each word, phrase, thought, and sentence of a pericope is digested, we should take the pulse of the implied readers and ask, What would their experience of the scene be at this moment? Hav-ing asked these sorts of questions moment by moment, we are able to get a sense of the conjectured changing experience of the implied readers as they move through a narrative or pas-sage and a sense of the overall effect the reading process would have had on them.

Example: Matthew 12:46–50
Identification with the Implied Readers

Since we are attempting to understand and identify with the experience of the implied reader, we begin with the assumption that the implied readers are reading the gospel of Matthew from beginning to end. By the time they come upon 12:46–50, they have already read 1:1–12:45 and carry impressions from this material with them into their reading of this passage. On the other hand, they have not read any of 13:1–28:20 and have only expectations (based on their prior knowledge of the non-Matthean story of the Christ event) of what is to come.

Because of the way the gospel of Matthew uses scripture and because of the heavy concentration on the conflicts be-tween traditional Jewish life and the new Christian way of life, many scholars argue that Matthew's implied readers were Jew-ish Christians.

Experience of the Implied Readers

Having submitted to the identity of the implied reader, we are ready to begin the process of reading while constantly taking our pulse. We take stock of ourselves as we ingest each movement of the passage:

While he was still speaking to the crowds,	The narrator introduces the scene by connecting it with the preceding scenes where (as we have seen) Jesus has been in conflict. Reading these opening words, the implied reader might expect that conflict to continue.
his mother and his brothers were standing outside, wanting to speak to him.	The expectation of conflict would lessen with the introduction of Jesus' family into the scene. Although this is Matthew's first mention of Jesus' brothers, the reader has already been introduced to Mary in the infancy narrative. The fact that an angel of the Lord defended Mary to Joseph and described her giving birth to Jesus as a fulfillment of scripture (1:20–22) gives the implied reader a strong positive image of her (and thus of her other children with her).
Someone told him, "Look, your mother and your brothers are standing outside, wanting to speak to you."	Since the character who speaks here is anonymous (instead of being an opponent or a follower) and his speech provides the reader with no new information, the implied reader's experience of the text is not altered greatly at this point. The speech allows the reader the opportunity to assume that Jesus will have a positive response to his mother and brothers similar to our own.
But to the one who had told him this, Jesus replied,	The use of the conjunction *but* immediately establishes in the reader a sense that what is to follow will be contrary to

what has preceded. The reader now suspects that the previous expectation needs to be modified.

"Who is my mother, and who are my brothers?"

The implied reader's suspicion is confirmed. Jesus has not identified with his family as the reader expected. Instead, he has asked an almost nonsensical question that moves the reader to desire an explanation. The reader, however, has been given no clues with which to predict the content of that explanation. The reader is drawn into the short scene by having his or her expectations overturned twice and by having her or his curiosity piqued concerning what Jesus will say next.

And pointing to his disciples,

The reference to the disciples would catch the implied reader off guard. Since the disciples have been present in so many scenes throughout Matthew up to this point, the reader might well assume they are present. But Jesus' turn to them is abrupt. There has been no mention of them previously in this scene and no foreshadowing that they were to appear. This shift would have been impossible to anticipate.

he said, "Here are my mother and my brothers!

Jesus' answer to his own question would surprise the implied reader. It would also leave him or her wanting (and expecting) a rationale for the substitution of disciples for blood relatives as "family."

For whoever does the will of my Father in heaven is my brother and sister and mother."

The expectation for such a rationale is fulfilled by Jesus. In this closing statement Jesus redefines both family and disciples. Of all the characters in the gospel, it can be assumed that the implied reader, as a first century Christian, would most closely identify with the disciples. Therefore, the resolution of the scene could provoke numerous types of responses depending on how strongly the individual implied reader identified with the disciples. For example: (1) The implied reader might have a sense of pride, joy, or fulfillment at the idea of being recognized as part of Jesus' own family. (2) The language of being in Jesus' family might strengthen the implied reader's emotional tie with other Christians, since he or she has already heard Jesus refer to members of the community of faith as "brothers and sisters" (5:22, 23, 47; cf. 5:44). (3) From a different angle, the implied reader might question whether she or he has been doing the will of God, and thus whether or not she or he is part of Jesus' family (i.e., whether she or he is a true disciple). (4) If the implied reader assumes that Jesus is a model for authentic existence in the faith, then this scene would be viewed as a confirmation of Jesus' earlier comments about the divisions that people of faith would experience in their own families (10:21, 35–37). And thus, again, we see that Jesus' pronouncement could be experienced by the implied reader as either call or comfort. How the implied reader would respond to this continuing emphasis would depend on his or her own experience with family after conversion.

Although we have not exhausted all possible responses to Matthew 12:46–50, we have illustrated the point that narratives are, by nature, multivalent. Meaning cannot be separated from the reader's experience, and thus there are as many possible readings as there are readers themselves. The type of response evoked by a narrative is dependent on the social, economic, and historical location of the reader. By focusing on the *implied* reader (an ideal reader, as some refer to the role), we have considerably narrowed the range of responses we consider during our exegetical process, but even this focus does not lead to a single interpretation.

For Further Reading

Detweiler, Robert, ed. *Reader Response Approaches to Biblical and Secular Texts. Semeia* 31 (1985).

Fowler, Robert M. "Reader-Response Criticism: Figuring Mark's Reader." In *Mark & Method: New Approaches in Biblical Studies*, ed. Janice Capel Anderson and Stephen D. Moore. 50–83. Minneapolis: Fortress Press, 1992.

_____. *Let the Reader Understand: Reader Response Criticism and the Gospel of Mark.* Minneapolis, Fortress Press, 1991.

Lategan, Bernard C. "Reader Response Theory." In *The Anchor Bible Dictionary*, ed. David Noel Freedman, 5.625–28. New York: Doubleday, 1992.

McKnight, Edgar V. *Postmodern Use of the Bible: The Emergence of Reader-Oriented Criticism.* Nashville: Abingdon Press, 1988

_____, ed. *Reader Perspectives on the New Testament. Semeia* 48 (1989).

_____. "Reader-Response Criticism." In *To Each Its Own Meaning: An Introduction to Biblical Criticisms and Their Application*, ed. Steven L. McKenzie and Stephen R. Haynes, 1st ed., 197–219. Louisville, Ky.: Westminster/John Knox Press, 1993.

Moore, Stephen D. "Stories of Reading: Doing Gospel Criticism as/with a Reader." In *Literary Criticism and the Gospels: The Theoretical Challenge*, 71–107. New Haven/London: Yale University Press, 1989.

Resseguie, James L. "Reader-Response Criticism and the Synoptic Gospels." *Journal of the American Academy of Religion* 52 (1984): 307–24.

Sanders, E. P., and Margaret Davies. "Rhetorical Criticism and the 'Implied Reader.'" In *Studying the Synoptic Gospels*, 240–51. London/Philadelphia: SCM/Trinity Press International, 1989.